Depression

DATE DUE

MAR 2 2 2016			
	MAR 2 4 2016		

Demco, Inc. 38-293

Depression

Other Books of Related Interest:

Opposing Viewpoints Series
Alternative Medicine

Medicine

Mental Illness

Current Controversies
Mental Health

Suicide

At Issue Series
Are Americans Overmedicated?

Physician-Assisted Suicide

Depression

Emma Carlson Berne, Book Editor

GREENHAVEN PRESS
An imprint of Thomson Gale, a part of The Thomson Corporation

THOMSON

GALE

Detroit • New York • San Francisco • New Haven, Conn. • Waterville, Maine • London

10|07

131065160

Christine Nasso, *Publisher*
Elizabeth Des Chenes, *Managing Editor*

© 2007 The Gale Group.

Star logo is a trademark and Gale and Greenhaven Press are registered trademarks used herein under license.

For more information, contact:
Greenhaven Press
27500 Drake Rd.
Farmington Hills, MI 48331-3535
Or you can visit our Internet site at http://www.gale.com

LIBRARY OF CONGRESS CATALOGING-IN-PUBLICATION DATA

Depression / Emma Carlson Berne, book editor.
p. cm. -- (Contemporary issues companion)
Includes bibliographical references and index.
ISBN-13: 978-0-7377-3645-8 (hardcover)
ISBN-13: 978-0-7377-2451-6 (pbk.)
1. Depression, Mental. 2. Depression, Mental--Treatment. I. Berne, Emma Carlson.
RC537.D425 2007
616.85'27--dc22

2007019643

ISBN-10: 0-7377-3645-3 (hardcover)
ISBN-10: 0-7377-2451-X (pbk.)

Printed in the United States of America
10 9 8 7 6 5 4 3 2 1

Contents

Foreword   **7**

Introduction   **10**

Chapter 1: What Is Depression?

1. Depression Is a Serious Mental Illness   **15**
   Margaret Strock

2. Dysthymia: A Lasting Depressed Mood   **24**
   Harvard Mental Health Letter

3. Depression Through History   **31**
   Dan G. Blazer

4. Depression's Role in Bodily Disease   **40**
   Marianne Szegedy-Maszak

5. Depression and Suicide   **46**
   Joanne Kenen

6. Understanding Postpartum Depression   **59**
   Mark Levy and Stacy Sabraw

Chapter 2: Personal Perspectives on Depression

1. Motherhood and Depression   **69**
   Kathryn Harrison

2. The Relief of Medication   **77**
   John Falk

3. A Story of Teenage Depression   **86**
   David L. Marcus

4. My Experience with Deep Brain Stimulation   **97**
   David Beresford

Chapter 3: Treatments for Depression

1. An Overview of Alternative Therapies   **104**
   Aviva Patz

2. Varieties of Psychotherapy   **114**
   Harvard Women's Health Watch

3. Omega-3s and Depression   **120**
   Patrick Perry

4. Understanding Transcranial Magnetic Stimulation   **127**
   Dennis O'Brien

Chapter 4: The Debate over Antidepressants

1. The History of Antidepressants   **135**
   David Healy

2. Current Antidepressants Are Flawed but Needed   **146**
   Apoorva Mandavilli

3. Antidepressants' Link to Adolescent Suicide   **155**
   Jennifer Barrett Ozols

4. Controversy over Medicating Depression   **161**
   Peter D. Kramer

Organizations to Contact   **170**

Bibliography   **175**

Index   **180**

Foreword

In the news, on the streets, and in neighborhoods, individuals are confronted with a variety of social problems. Such problems may affect people directly: A young woman may struggle with depression, suspect a friend of having bulimia, or watch a loved one battle cancer. And even the issues that do not directly affect her private life—such as religious cults, domestic violence, or legalized gambling—still impact the larger society in which she lives. Discovering and analyzing the complexities of issues that encompass communal and societal realms as well as the world of personal experience is a valuable educational goal in the modern world.

Effectively addressing social problems requires familiarity with a constantly changing stream of data. Becoming well informed about today's controversies is an intricate process that often involves reading myriad primary and secondary sources, analyzing political debates, weighing various experts' opinions—even listening to firsthand accounts of those directly affected by the issue. For students and general observers, this can be a daunting task because of the sheer volume of information available in books, periodicals, on the evening news, and on the Internet. Researching the consequences of legalized gambling, for example, might entail sifting through congressional testimony on gambling's societal effects, examining private studies on Indian gaming, perusing numerous Web sites devoted to Internet betting, and reading essays written by lottery winners as well as interviews with recovering compulsive gamblers. Obtaining valuable information can be time-consuming—since it often requires researchers to pore over numerous documents and commentaries before discovering a source relevant to their particular investigation.

Greenhaven's Contemporary Issues Companion series seeks to assist this process of research by providing readers with

useful and pertinent information about today's complex issues. Each volume in this anthology series focuses on a topic
of current interest, presenting informative and thought-
provoking selections written from a wide variety of view-
points. The readings selected by the editors include such di-
verse sources as personal accounts and case studies, pertinent
factual and statistical articles, and relevant commentaries and
over views. This diversity of sources and views, found in every Contemporary Issues Companion, offers readers a broad
perspective in one convenient volume.

In addition, each title in the Contemporary Issues Companion series is designed especially for young adults. The selections included in every volume are chosen for their accessibility and are expertly edited in consideration of both the
reading and comprehension levels of the audience. The structure of the anthologies also enhances accessibility. An intro-
ductory essay places each issue in context and provides helpful
facts such as historical background or current statistics and
legislation that pertain to the topic. The chapters that follow
organize the material and focus on specific aspects of the
book's topic. Every essay is introduced by a brief summary of
its main points and biographical information about the author. These summaries aid in comprehension and can also
serve to direct readers to material of immediate interest and
need. Finally, a comprehensive index allows readers to effi-
ciently scan and locate content.

The Contemporary Issues Companion series is an ideal
launching point for research on a particular topic. Each anthology in the series is composed of readings taken from an
extensive gamut of resources, including periodicals, newspapers, books, government documents, the publications of private and public organizations, and Internet websites. In these
volumes, readers will find factual support suitable for use in
reports, debates, speeches, and research papers. The antholo-

gies also facilitate further research, featuring a book and periodical bibliography and a list of organizations to contact for additional information.

A perfect resource for both students and the general reader, Greenhaven's Contemporary Issues Companion series is sure to be a valued source of current, readable information on social problems that interest young adults. It is the editors' hope that readers will find the Contemporary Issues Companion series useful as a starting point to formulate their own opinions about and answers to the complex issues of the present day.

Introduction

Depression as a mental illness is complex, common, and poorly understood—an unfortunate combination of factors for the 20.9 million Americans who suffer from it during any one-year period, according to the National Institutes of Mental Health. The illness has been understood variously over the centuries. Those suffering from depression have been seen as weak, lazy, or infected by the devil; have been denied medical care and health benefits; and have been accused of being a burden on society. Only relatively recently has depression been viewed for what it is: a legitimate mental illness that requires medical evaluation and treatment.

The condition fascinates people. Of all mental illnesses, few have been more thoroughly discussed, portrayed, and pondered than depression. The co-occurrence of the illness and creativity, for instance, has been long noted; the composer Beethoven, the impressionist painter Vincent Van Gogh, the Victorian poet Alfred, Lord Tennyson, and the twentieth-century American author Sylvia Plath are just a few examples of artists who have suffered from the disease. Depressive characters also appear frequently in literature. Shakespeare's Hamlet, for instance, distraught over his father's murder and mother's treachery, presents a strikingly realistic portrait of a depressed person. Ebenezer Scrooge, from Charles Dickens's *A Christmas Carol*, exhibits some signs of the illness, as well.

Modern medical research and study of the physiology of the brain have contributed empirical data that shed light on depression and its causes. Increasingly, depression is being viewed as a physical illness, rather than a metaphysical one, with effects on the health and longevity of sufferers.

Despite their limited scientific knowledge, though, some early physicians did recognize depression—or melancholy, as it was historically called—as some sort of medical problem, rather than a defect in the moral or spiritual state of the patient. One of these was the English physician and clergyman Robert Burton (1577–1640), who suffered from depression himself. In 1621, he wrote *The Anatomy of Melancholy*, the first book in Western literature to discuss the disorder in medical terms.

Medieval medicine, which Burton inherited, continued to be based on the idea of the four humors, a theory attributed to the Greek physician Hippocrates (ca. B.C. 460–ca. B.C. 370). This theory asserted that four fluids in the body regulate temperament and health. Melancholy was caused by an excess of black bile, Burton believed. More importantly, he noted, melancholy was a painful and serious disease. "Some make a question whether the diseases of the mind or body be more grievous, but there is no comparison, no doubt to be made of it, the diseases of the mind are far more grievous . . . body and soul is misaffected here but the soul especially," he wrote.

For all his understanding of depression, Burton still separated the diseases of the mind from those of the body. This distinction persisted through the eighteenth and nineteenth centuries until the rise of modern psychiatry, the medical study of the brain, and other scientific advancements in the early twentieth century, which tended to analyze depression as a physiological phenomenon.

Researchers in the 1950s discovered that certain chemicals in the brain, called neurotransmitters, were responsible for regulating mood and emotion. In 1965, psychiatrist Joseph Schildkraut hypothesized that depression was caused by an imbalance of these chemicals, in particular the mood-affecting norepinephrine and serotonin. Schildkraut's research and that of others in the field eventually led to the creation of selective serotonin reuptake inhibitor (SSRI) antidepressants.

The theory of chemical imbalances became widely accepted in the medical community. Depression sufferers and their families were relieved to have a physical explanation for their often confusing, upsetting symptoms. Some in the medical community have cautioned that the "chemical imbalance" theory has been oversimplified, but few would deny that the perception of depression had moved another step into the physical realm.

Evidence that depression may be a risk factor in the development of other bodily diseases such as stroke, diabetes, and heart disease further connects the mental illness to overall physical health. Dwight Evans, a psychiatrist from the University of Pennsylvania, was quoted by *U.S. News and World Report* as saying: "[There] is also considerable recent evidence that mood disorders can affect the course of medical illnesses. It goes both ways. Depression may be both a cause and a consequence of medical illness."

In 2004 *New Scientist* reported that researchers at St. Louis's Washington University had found that patients who suffered bouts of major depression exhibited brain damage in a portion of the brain called the hippocampus, which relates to memory. Further exploration showed damage to the prefrontal cortex, which regulates thoughts and actions and the fear center, the amygdala. "Depression," *New Scientist* writer Peter Farley noted, "the major symptoms of which were still largely described in psychological terms, was suddenly seen to share features with serious neurodegenerative diseases such as Parkinson's and Alzheimer's." These discoveries have prompted some scientists to speculate that depression may move from a psychological classification to a physical one, a change that may produce better treatment options.

Despite significant medical advances, depression continues to baffle in its complexities and permutations. Its effects can reach into the home, workplace, and public sector, affecting those of every age, gender, ethnicity, and social class. In order to illuminate key aspects of this important subject, *Contemporary Issues Companion: Depression* identifies some of the causes and symptoms of depression, offers narratives from depression sufferers, provides an overview of treatment, and discusses the controversy over use of antidepressants.

CHAPTER 1

What Is Depression?

Depression Is a Serious Mental Illness

Margaret Strock

In the following excerpt from a pamphlet put out by the National Institute of Mental Health (NIMH), mental health writer Margaret Strock provides a general overview of depressive illnesses, their symptoms, treatments, and effects on men, women, children, and the elderly. Depression is common in the United States, Strock explains, and has different forms, each of which has its own set of symptoms and treatments. In addition, depression manifests itself in various ways among groups: women, for instance, tend to experience depression differently than men. Though the illness is common, Strock writes, people can be reluctant to seek treatment, sometimes for fear they will appear weak. Margaret Strock writes on health subjects for the Public Communication and Information Branch of the NIMH, a federal agency, which is a division of the National Institutes of Health.

In any given 1-year period, 9.5 percent of the population, or about 18.8 million American adults, suffer from a depressive illness. The economic cost for this disorder is high, but the cost in human suffering cannot be estimated. Depressive illnesses often interfere with normal functioning and cause pain and suffering not only to those who have a disorder, but also to those who care about them. Serious depression can destroy family life as well as the life of the ill person. But much of this suffering is unnecessary.

Most people with a depressive illness do not seek treatment, although the great majority, even those whose depression is extremely severe can be helped. Thanks to years of fruitful research, there are now medications and psychosocial

Margaret Strock, "Plain Talk About Depression," *National Institute of Mental Health*, May 11, 2006. Reproduced by permission.

therapies such as cognitive/behavioral, "talk," or interpersonal that ease the pain of depression.

Unfortunately, many people do not recognize that depression is a treatable illness. If you feel that you or someone you care about is one of the many undiagnosed depressed people in this country, the information presented here may help you take the steps that may save your own or someone else's life.

Defining Depressive Disorders

A depressive disorder is an illness that involves the body, mood, and thoughts. It affects the way a person eats and sleeps, the way one feels about oneself, and the way one thinks about things. A depressive disorder is not the same as a passing blue mood. It is not a sign of personal weakness or a condition that can be willed or wished away. People with a depressive illness cannot merely "pull themselves together" and get better. Without treatment, symptoms can last for weeks, months, or years. Appropriate treatment, however, can help most people who suffer from depression.

Depressive disorders come in different forms, just as is the case with other illnesses such as heart disease. This pamphlet briefly describes three of the most common types of depressive disorders. However, within these types there are variations in the number of symptoms, their severity, and persistence.

Major depression is manifested by a combination of symptoms that interfere with the ability to work, study, sleep, eat, and enjoy once pleasurable activities. Such a disabling episode of depression may occur only once but more commonly occurs several times in a lifetime.

A less severe type of depression, dysthymia, involves long-term, chronic symptoms that do not disable, but keep one from functioning well or from feeling good. Many people with dysthymia also experience major depressive episodes at some time in their lives.

Another type of depression is bipolar disorder, also called manic-depressive illness. Not nearly as prevalent as other forms of depressive disorders, bipolar disorder is characterized by cycling mood changes: severe highs (mania) and lows (depression). Sometimes the mood switches are dramatic and rapid, but most often they are gradual. When in the depressed cycle, an individual can have any or all of the symptoms of a depressive disorder. When in the manic cycle, the individual may be overactive, overtalkative, and have a great deal of energy. Mania often affects thinking, judgment, and social behavior in ways that cause serious problems and embarrassment. For example, the individual in a manic phase may feel elated, full of grand schemes that might range from unwise business decisions to romantic sprees. Mania, left untreated, may worsen to a psychotic state.

Symptoms of Depression and Mania

Not everyone who is depressed or manic experiences every symptom. Some people experience a few symptoms, some many. Severity of symptoms varies with individuals and also varies over time.

Depression

- Persistent sad, anxious, or "empty" mood

- Feelings of hopelessness, pessimism

- Feelings of guilt, worthlessness, helplessness

- Loss of interest or pleasure in hobbies and activities that were once enjoyed, including sex

- Decreased energy, fatigue, being "slowed down"

- Difficulty concentrating, remembering, making decisions

- Insomnia, early-morning awakening, or oversleeping

- Appetite and/or weight loss or overeating and weight gain
- Thoughts of death or suicide; suicide attempts
- Restlessness, irritability
- Persistent physical symptoms that do not respond to treatment, such as headaches, digestive disorders, and chronic pain

Mania

- Abnormal or excessive elation
- Unusual irritability
- Decreased need for sleep
- Grandiose notions
- Increased talking
- Racing thoughts
- Increased sexual desire
- Markedly increased energy
- Poor judgment
- Inappropriate social behavior

Causes of Depression

Some types of depression run in families, suggesting that a biological vulnerability can be inherited. This seems to be the case with bipolar disorder. Studies of families in which members of each generation develop bipolar disorder found that those with the illness have a somewhat different genetic makeup than those who do not get ill. However, the reverse is not true: Not everybody with the genetic makeup that causes vulnerability to bipolar disorder will have the illness. Apparently additional factors, possibly stresses at home, work, or school, are involved in its onset.

In some families, major depression also seems to occur generation after generation. However, it can also occur in people who have no family history of depression. Whether inherited or not, major depressive disorder is often associated with changes in brain structures or brain function.

People who have low self-esteem, who consistently view themselves and the world with pessimism or who are readily overwhelmed by stress, are prone to depression. Whether this represents a psychological predisposition or an early form of the illness is not clear.

[Since the 1990s], researchers have shown that physical changes in the body can be accompanied by mental changes as well. Medical illnesses such as stroke, a heart attack, cancer, Parkinson's disease, and hormonal disorders can cause depressive illness, making the sick person apathetic and unwilling to care for his or her physical needs, thus prolonging the recovery period. Also, a serious loss, difficult relationship, financial problem, or any stressful (unwelcome or even desired) change in life patterns can trigger a depressive episode. Very often, a combination of genetic, psychological, and environmental factors is involved in the onset of a depressive disorder. Later episodes of illness typically are precipitated by only mild stresses, or none at all.

Depression in Women

Women experience depression about twice as often as men. Many hormonal factors may contribute to the increased rate of depression in women, particularly such factors as menstrual cycle changes, pregnancy, miscarriage, postpartum period [after birth], pre-menopause, and menopause. Many women also face additional stresses such as responsibilities both at work and home, single parenthood, and caring for children and for aging parents.children and for aging parents.

A recent NIMH [National Institute of Mental Health] study showed that in the case of severe premenstrual syndrome (PMS), women with a preexisting vulnerability to PMS experienced relief from mood and physical symptoms when their sex hormones were suppressed. Shortly after the hormones were reintroduced, they again developed symptoms of PMS. Women without a history of PMS reported no effects of the hormonal manipulation.

Many women are also particularly vulnerable after the birth of a baby. The hormonal and physical changes, as well as the added responsibility of a new life, can be factors that lead to postpartum depression in some women. While transient "blues" are common in new mothers, a full-blown depressive episode is not a normal occurrence and requires active intervention. Treatment by a sympathetic physician and the family's emotional support for the new mother are prime considerations in aiding her to recover her physical and mental well-being and her ability to care for and enjoy the infant.

Depression in Men

Although men are less likely to suffer from depression than women, three to four million men in the United States are affected by the illness. Men are less likely to admit to depression, and doctors are less likely to suspect it. The rate of suicide in men is four times that of women, though more women attempt it. In fact, after age 70, the rate of men's suicide rises, reaching a peak after age 85.

Depression can also affect the physical health in men differently from women. A new study shows that, although depression is associated with an increased risk of coronary heart disease in both men and women, only men suffer a high death rate.

Men's depression is often masked by alcohol or drugs, or by the socially acceptable habit of working excessively long hours. Depression typically shows up in men not as feeling hopeless and helpless, but as being irritable, angry, and discouraged; hence, depression may be difficult to recognize as such in men. Even if a man realizes that he is depressed, he may be less willing than a woman to seek help. Encouragement and support from concerned family members can make a difference. In the workplace, employee assistance professionals or worksite mental health programs can be of assistance in helping men understand and accept depression as a real illness that needs treatment.

Depression in the Elderly

Some people have the mistaken idea that it is normal for the elderly to feel depressed. On the contrary, most older people feel satisfied with their lives. Sometimes, though, when depression develops, it may be dismissed as a normal part of aging. Depression in the elderly, undiagnosed and untreated, causes needless suffering for the family and for the individual who could otherwise live a fruitful life. When he or she does go to the doctor, the symptoms described are usually physical, for the older person is often reluctant to discuss feelings of hopelessness, sadness, loss of interest in normally pleasurable activities, or extremely prolonged grief after a loss.

Recognizing how depressive symptoms in older people are often missed, many health care professionals are learning to identify and treat the underlying depression. They recognize that some symptoms may be side effects of medication the older person is taking for a physical problem, or they may be caused by a co-occurring illness. If a diagnosis of depression is made, treatment with medication and/or psychotherapy will help the depressed person return to a happier, more fulfilling life. Recent research suggests that brief psychotherapy (talk therapies that help a person in day-to-day relationships or in learning to counter the distorted negative thinking that commonly accompanies depression) is effective in reducing symptoms in short-term depression in older persons who are medically ill. Psychotherapy is also useful in older patients who cannot or will not take medication. Efficacy studies show that late-life depression can be treated with psychotherapy.

Improved recognition and treatment of depression in late life will make those years more enjoyable and fulfilling for the depressed elderly person, the family, and caretakers.

Depression in Children

Only [since the 1980s] has depression in children been taken very seriously. The depressed child may pretend to be sick, refuse to go to school, cling to a parent, or worry that the parent may die. Older children may sulk, get into trouble at school, be negative, grouchy, and feel misunderstood. Because normal behaviors vary from one childhood stage to another, it can be difficult to tell whether a child is just going through a temporary "phase" or is suffering from depression. Sometimes the parents become worried about how the child's behavior has changed, or a teacher mentions that "your child doesn't seem to be himself." In such a case, if a visit to the child's pediatrician rules out physical symptoms, the doctor will probably suggest that the child be evaluated, preferably by a psychiatrist who specializes in the treatment of children. If treatment is needed, the doctor may suggest that another therapist, usually a social worker or a psychologist, provide therapy while the psychiatrist will oversee medication if it is needed. Parents should not be afraid to ask questions: What are the therapist's qualifications? What kind of therapy will the child have? Will the family as a whole participate in therapy? Will my child's therapy include an antidepressant? If so, what might the side effects be?

The National Institute of Mental Health (NIMH) has identified the use of medications for depression in children as an important area for research. The NIMH-supported Research Units on Pediatric Psychopharmacology (RUPPs) form a network of seven research sites where clinical studies on the effects of medications for mental disorders can be conducted in children and adolescents. Among the medications being studied are antidepressants, some of which have been found to be effective in treating children with depression, if properly monitored by the child's physician.

Dysthymia: A Lasting Depressed Mood

Harvard Mental Health Letter

The Harvard Mental Health Letter *is a monthly newsletter written by staff at the Harvard Medical School. It provides information for both professionals and laypeople on a wide range of mental health topics, including disorders, treatments, and current research. In the following selection, the author provides an overview of dysthymia, which is a depressed mood lasting more than two years. Dysthymia is often mistakenly called "minor" depression, the author explains, because those suffering from it are still able to function at work and home, despite persistent depressive symptoms. It is a serious illness, however, and should be treated with drugs, psychotherapy, or a combination. Many people do not even realize they are suffering from dysthymia, though, which is a major obstacle to their obtaining treatment. Family doctors can assist in detection, the author writes, by being aware of and alert to the sometimes subtle dysthymic symptoms.*

Depression is a word with many meanings—anything from a passing mood of sadness or discouragement to a condition of inconsolable misery, suicidal thoughts, and even delusions as well as severe physical symptoms. It's regarded as a clinical disorder when depressed mood and related symptoms are serious enough or last long enough to interfere with work, social life, family life, or physical health.

The Greek word dysthymia means "bad state of mind" or "ill humor." As one of the two chief forms of clinical depression, it usually has fewer or less serious symptoms than major

Harvard Mental Health Letter, "Dysthymia," vol. 21, February 2005. © 2005 President and Fellows of Harvard College. Republished with permission of Harvard Health Publications.

depression but lasts longer. The American Psychiatric Association defines dysthymia as depressed mood most of the time for at least two years, along with at least two of the following symptoms: poor appetite or overeating; insomnia or excessive sleep; low energy or fatigue; low self-esteem; poor concentration or indecisiveness; and hopelessness.

Dysthymia and major depression naturally have many symptoms in common, including depressed mood, disturbed sleep, low energy, and poor concentration. There are also parallel symptoms: poor appetite, low self-esteem, and hopelessness in dysthymia, corresponding to the more severe symptoms of weight change, excessive guilt, and thoughts of death or suicide in major depression. Major depression may also include two symptoms not found in the standard definition of dysthymia: anhedonia (inability to feel pleasure) and psychomotor symptoms (chiefly lethargy or agitation). An episode of major depression requires at least five symptoms instead of three, but it need last only two weeks rather than two years.

Dysthymia is a serious disorder. It is not "minor" depression, and it is not a condition intermediate between severe clinical depression and depression in the casual colloquial sense. In some cases it is more disabling than major depression. Still, dysthymia as currently described is so similar to major depression that the American Psychiatric Association's diagnostic manual also suggests, as a possibility for further investigation, an alternative definition with symptoms including anhedonia, social withdrawal, guilt, and irritability but not appetite or sleep disturbance. The purpose is to distinguish dysthymia more clearly from major depression by emphasizing mood and personal relations over physical symptoms.

Dysthymia is about as common as major depression. Its chronic nature makes it one of the disorders most often seen by psychotherapists. About 6% of the population of the United States has had an episode of dysthymia at some time, 3% in the last year. As many as a third of patients in psychotherapy may be suffering from dysthymia. Like major depression, it is more common in women than in men, but it tends to arise earlier in life. The American Psychiatric Association distinguishes between this early-onset form and a form that occurs later in life and often comes on less gradually.

More than half of people with dysthymia eventually have an episode of major depression, and about half of patients treated for major depression are suffering from this double depression. Many patients who recover partially from major depression also have milder symptoms that persist for years. This type of chronic depression is difficult to distinguish from dysthymia.

Is There a Depressive Personality?

In principle, personality is usually lifelong, while moods come and go. But dysthymia, as now defined, has to last longer than any other psychiatric disorder in the manual. That can make it difficult to distinguish from a personality disorder—especially the group that includes avoidant, dependent, and obsessive-compulsive personality, with their symptoms of timidity, excessive worry, helplessness, and social withdrawal.

Some would prefer to speak of a depressive personality disorder instead. That diagnosis was removed from the official manual in 1980 but has been reintroduced as a possible topic of investigation. The proposed symptoms include a strong tendency to be critical of oneself and others, pessimism, guilt, brooding, and gloominess. Anhedonia and physical symptoms are not part of the definition, but this personality disorder otherwise has a great deal in common with dysthymia.

Mood and personality are the emotional weather and emotional climate of individuals, so the symptoms of mood and personality disorders naturally overlap. The thought schemas that cognitive therapists find at the roots of major depression and dysthymia—certain beliefs about the self, the world, and the future—are also the basis of depressive personality. Disturbances in mood can have effects on a person's emotional state and social life that resemble a personality disorder. And people are more easily demoralized and recover more slowly from any stress or misfortune if they are pessimistic and self-critical by nature—or emotionally unstable, impulsive, and hypersensitive to loss.

Looking for Causes

Like major depression, dysthymia has roots in genetic susceptibility, neurochemical imbalances, childhood and adult stress and trauma, and social circumstances, especially isolation and the unavailability of help. Depression that begins as a mood fluctuation may deepen and persist when equilibrium cannot be restored because of poor internal regulation or external stress.

Dysthymia runs in families and probably has a hereditary component. The rate of depression in the families of people with dysthymia is as high as 50% for the early-onset form of the disorder. There are few twin or adoption studies, so it's uncertain how much of this family connection is genetic. Nearly half of people with dysthymia have a symptom that also occurs in major depression, shortened REM latency—that is, they start rapid eye movement (vivid dreaming) sleep unusually early in the night.

The stress that provokes dysthymia, at least the early-onset form, is usually chronic rather than acute. Studies show that it usually has a gradual onset and does not follow distinct upsetting events. In old age, dysthymia is more likely to be the result of physical disability, medical illness, cognitive decline, or bereavement. In some older men, low testosterone may also be a factor. Physical brain trauma—concussions and the like—can also have surprising long-term effects on mood that often take the form of dysthymia.

At least three-quarters of patients with dysthymia also have a chronic physical illness or another psychiatric disorder such as one of the anxiety disorders, drug addiction, or alcoholism. In these cases, it is difficult to distinguish the original cause, especially when there is a vicious cycle in which, say, depression exacerbates alcoholism or heart disease exacerbates depression.

The same vicious cycle exists in many other situations. For a person who is vulnerable to depression, every problem seems more difficult to solve and every misfortune causes more suffering. Depressed people give discouraging interpretations to every event in their lives, and these interpretations make them still more depressed. Depression often alienates others, and the resulting isolation and low social support make the symptoms worse. The experience of chronic depression may sensitize the brain to stress, heightening its vulnerability to further depression.

Treatment

Most people with dysthymia are undertreated. They usually see only their family doctors, who often fail to diagnose the problem. They may only complain about physical symptoms, or fail to complain at all became the disorder has become so much a part of them that they believe that is simply how life is. In older people, dysthymia may be disguised as dementia, apathy, or irritability.

A physician might ask an open question like, "How are things at home?"—follow with, "Have you been feeling down, depressed, or sad?"—then go on to ask whether the symptoms have affected a patient's home life, work, or personal relations. There are also several brief screening questionnaires. If the answers suggest dysthymia, a standard clinical interview can be used to confirm the diagnosis.

Like major depression, dysthymia is treated with psychotherapy and medications—usually the same medications and the same kinds of psychotherapy. The most common drug treatments today are selective serotonin reuptake inhibitors like fluoxetine (Prozac) and sertraline (Zoloft), or one of the newer dual action antidepressants such as venlafaxine (Effexor). Some patients may do better with a tricyclic antidepressant like imipramine (Tofranil).

Supportive therapy provides advice, reassurance, sympathy, and education about the disorder. Cognitive therapy identifies and corrects thought patterns that promote self-defeating attitudes. Behavioral treatment improves social skills and teaches ways to manage stress and unlearn learned helplessness. Psychodynamic therapy helps patients resolve emotional conflicts, especially those derived from childhood experience. Interpersonal therapy helps patients cope with personal disputes, loss and separation, and transitions between social roles.

Drugs or Psychotherapy?

A 2003 review of controlled research found that medication is slightly superior to psychotherapy in the treatment of dysthymia. But a statistical difference among a large number of patients in many different situations is not necessarily a guide for any individual case. Some patients—especially older people—will not or cannot take drugs, sometimes because of side effects or drug interactions. For many others, a combination of long-term psychotherapy and medication may be most effective. A solid relationship with a psychotherapist or other professional can be important in maintaining a willingness to continue medications.

Recovery from dysthymia often takes a long time, and the symptoms often return. One study found that 70% recovered in an average of about four years, and 50% had a recurrence. Another study found an average time to recurrence of nearly six years. After recovery, many patients find it helpful to continue doing whatever made them well—whether it was a drug or psychotherapy.

While the search continues for better drugs and better forms of psychotherapy, the problem remains that, despite

much improvement in recent years, most people with dysthymia are not receiving even the imperfect available treatments. Even when they do see professionals, they may not fill
their prescriptions or take their drugs consistently, and they
may abandon psychotherapy too soon.

A recent study based on a telephone survey of more than
800 adults with dysthymia found that only 20% had seen a
mental health professional; only one-quarter had received any
medication and only one-third some kind of counseling, usually brief. And [during the 1990s] a survey commissioned by
the National Depressive and Manic Depressive Association
(now the Depression and Bipolar Support Alliance) found
that doctors and patients often communicate poorly about the
symptoms and treatment. Patients may stop taking drugs because they do not receive enough information about side effects or routine follow-up visits. For both the public and professionals, what is most important today may be recognizing
that dysthymia is a treatable disorder, identifying it, and following through.

Depression Through History

Dan G. Blazer

Dan G. Blazer is a professor of psychiatry at Duke University. In the following excerpt from his book The Age of Melancholy, *Blazer traces cultural views on depression from ancient Greeks through the Renaissance to the early twentieth century. For much of history, Blazer explains, depression was seen as an imbalance in humors—elements in the body—and was called "melancholy." Blazer identifies this idea as one of the chemical or biological schools of thought. In contrast, religion has historically seen depression as the presence of evil spirits or the absence of God. The chemical school surfaced again in twentieth-century America with the rise of modern psychiatry, Blazer points out, especially with relation to severe depression.*

Depression, a relative latecomer to the psychiatric nomenclature, was called "melancholia" before the 18th century and varied relatively little over the years in the original Hippocratic (460–357 B.C.) [Hippocrates was a Greek physician] assumptions about causes. Melancholia was the Latin transliteration of a Greek term meaning a mental disorder involving prolonged fear and sadness or depression. The symptoms also included aversion to food, sleeplessness, irritability and restlessness. Translated into English as "black bile" or "biliousness," a melancholic temperament was thought to be due to an excess of one of four humors (black bile, yellow bile, blood, and phlegm). [Greek physician] Aretaeus of Cappadocia (circa 150 A.D.) captured this view:

> If it [black bile] determined upwards to the stomach and diaphragm, it forms melancholy, for it produces flatulence and

eructations of the fetid and fishy nature, and it sends rumbling wind downwards and disturbs the understanding.

Though a theological view predominated as an explanation for melancholy in medieval Europe, the parallel view that sadness and despair were caused by aberrant bodily functions persisted. Throughout the Renaissance, writings about the passions increased and gradually escaped the purview of the theologians. Fear and sadness were usually the central features. During the 17th and 18th centuries, the term *melancholia* seemed gradually to have become restricted to a disease, whereas *melancholy* remained a synonym for *melancholia* and a popular term (with breadth and diffuseness of use much as *depression* is used today).

Physiologic explanations were increasingly employed after the Renaissance to explain the more severe varieties of melancholia. Despite his dualistic philosophy, [French philosopher René] Descartes (1596–1650) reaffirmed the traditional physiologic explanations for melancholia and introduced a mechanical etiologic [relating to the cause of disease] theory. Specifically, he thought that the animal spirits of the nervous system moved and agitated the brain to cause melancholia.

Alchemy and Humors

During the 17th and 18th centuries, chemical and mechanical explanations vied for supremacy. For example, [English physician] Richard Napier (1559–1634) dismissed the humoral theory for a wholehearted acceptance of alchemy as he developed an arsenal of chemical medicines. In contrast, Herman Hoerhaave (1668–1738) proposed that melancholia derived from sluggish flow of the blood and humors. Such mechanical theories did not hold sway, however, for they did little to change the existing approaches to therapy. The chemical theory was resurrected with a vengeance in the 20th century with the advent of effective chemicals (medications) to treat the symptoms of depression.

The 17th and 18th centuries produced two well-known popular authors who experienced recurrent episodes of depression. Robert Burton (1557–1640) first published *The Anatomy of Melancholy* in 1621. For Burton, melancholy was primarily the disease melancholia, even though he waxed eloquent in many literary genres to describe his experience with the malady. He suggested that the consensus definition was "*a kind of dotage without fever, having for his ordinary companions fear and sadness, without any apparent occasion.*" In his lengthy survey of the disorder, he believed the theory of humors to be central and an excess of black bile to be causative.

Burton was not unidimensional in his etiologic explanations. He developed a detailed description of a multicausal web that would do a 21st-century conceptual model proud. At the top of his hierarchy of causes he left sufficient (though not necessary) room for God and the devil to work their ways with the moods of men. In addition, he proposed more mundane contingent but not necessary life experiences to which persons might react with melancholia, including death of friends, loss of liberty, and poverty. He catalogued a host of biological causes, including external biological insults (such as a blow to the head) and internal bodily disorders (such as a "default of the spleen"). Burton thought heredity contributed to melancholy as well.

Health-related behaviors, such as eating a poor diet and sleeping too much, did not escape his attention. The irascible passions (shame, envy, malice) and concupiscible passions (desire of praise, pride, and love of learning) could also contribute. He was realistic and cautious regarding the difficulty in treating melancholy, though he prescribed social (e.g., be not solitary), psychological (e.g., confess grief to a friend), and physical (e.g., use leeches) therapies. Yet, as melancholia implies, "the name is imposed from the matter, and the disease denominated from the material cause."

Samuel Johnson (1709–1784) felt "overwhelmed with an horrible melancholia with perpetual irritation, fretfulness, and impatience; and with a dejection, gloom, and despair, which made existence misery." He considered his problem a disease of the mind for which there was no relief save the company of his friends. He also believed that this disposition of mind was inherited from his father. Johnson feared the malady would drive him insane. He also viewed his malady as coming from within. Though he became frustrated with his inability to overcome melancholia, he did not blame the cause of his problems on his behavior or his thoughts. The fault lay in his body, not his will. Johnson was also among the first to use the term *depression* in the English language to describe his mood. He wrote in 1761 that he was "under great depression."

The French alienist Jean-Philipe Esquirol (1772–1840) recognized the more severe forms of melancholy, which were expressed through psychotic thoughts and melancholic affect (a monomania [psychosis characterized by obsessive thoughts in one area] that he described as lypemania or sorrowful insanity). His work set the stage for other European psychiatrists to propose less severe states of melancholia without delusions, which were eventually categorized as simple melancholias. As these disorders were "affectively based," he set the stage for the Anglo-Saxon psychiatric term *affective disorder*.

Religious Melancholy

Despite physicians' focus on biological origins of melancholia from ancient times in Western civilization, another type of melancholia emerged within the Judeo-Christian world in parallel with "biliousness" [bad digestion, stomach pain, constipation, and flatulence]; namely, "religious melancholia." Depending in large part on the influence of the sacred in society, religious themes can be more or less dominant, yet among the religious the themes always have been present. For example, the centrality of religious melancholy was much greater in medieval Europe than during the Enlightenment.

Religious melancholy was prominent among the Puritans in America throughout the 18th century. That which renders religious melancholy of interest in this discussion is the perspective that severe episodes of melancholia were "reactions" to factors outside the body. The body was "visited" by a malignant spirit, often secondary to being abandoned by the Supreme Being for sinful behavior. Melancholy has been closely associated with spiritual life in many religions traditions; I focus on the Judeo-Christian tradition because it has had the strongest influence in Europe and North America.

The cause of religious melancholy might be direct from God as punishment for sin, direct from God for self-improvement as a purge of sins, or abandonment by God to the devil or demons. Each of these causes is implicit in the Hebrew Bible though it is difficult to read through our modern conceptions of depression without bias to accurately interpret the symptoms and causes of depression in scripture. King Saul experienced violent swings in his mood:

> Now the Spirit of the Lord had departed from Saul, and an evil spirit from the Lord tormented him. Saul's attendants said to him, "See, an evil spirit from God is tormenting you. Let our lord command his servants here to search for someone who can play the harp. He will play when the evil spirit from God comes upon you, and you will feel better." (1 Samuel 16:14–16).

David and Job

David, the harp player and later adversary of Saul, did little to assuage his mood swings. Saul eventually committed suicide. Given these symptoms and outcome, readers of the accounts of Saul for hundreds of years have interpreted his malady as manic-depressive illness, yet the writer of the scripture clearly identifies the origin of his malady as the actions of God. According to Richard Burton, in the *Anatomy of Melancholy*

(1661), "that God himself is a cause [of melancholy], for the punishment of sin, and satisfaction of justice, many examples & testimonies of holy Scriptures make evident unto us".

King David experienced depression while being pursued by Saul. He cried out to God,

> *Be merciful to me, O Lord, for I am in distress; my eyes grow weak with sorrow, my soul and my body with grief. My life is consumed by anguish and my years by groaning; my strength fails because of my affliction, and my bones grow weak. Because of all my enemies, I am the utter contempt of my neighbors; I am a dread to my friends—those who see me on the street flee from me. I am forgotten by them as though I were dead; I have become like broken pottery. For I hear the slander of many; there is terror on every side; they conspire against me and plot to take my life. (Psalms 31:9–13).*

Unlike Saul, David viewed his emotional suffering as resulting from the perils secondary to his service to God, perhaps contributing to his spiritual growth. He found hope toward the end of the psalm, despite his melancholy.

Job experienced severe despair, to the point of gladly receiving death if it were offered (though he refused to commit suicide):

> *May the day of my birth perish, and the night it was said, "A boy is born!" That day may it turn to darkness; may God above not care about it; may no light shine upon it. May darkness and deep shadow claim it once more; may a cloud settle over it; may blackness overwhelm its light. That night may thick darkness seize it; may it not be included among the days of the year nor be entered in any of the months. May that night be barren; may no shout of joy be heard in it. (Job 3:3–7).*

The writer clearly viewed melancholia as external to Job. Though the reason for his anguish was (and remains) unknown, the theme of God's abandoning Job is implicit throughout the narrative. Saul's, David's, and Job's melancholy all derived from a reaction to external circumstances.

Burton developed the theme of religious melancholy (and devoted a chapter to the topic). His experience with melancholia during the late Renaissance was compatible with the concept of the malady as a visitation on a person because he or she has wandered from the ways of God. Belief in God and the practice of religion were not the causes of melancholy. Religion was the fabric from which the lives of people in the 17th century were woven. Religion provided meaning through faith, a worldview that in turn provided answers to a set of ultimate and grounding questions. Rather, religious melancholy derived from religious excess or defect. In other words, religious aberration, such as deviation from the faith of one's community, could cause severe depression. Despite Burton's interest in the humors, he could not ignore the social context of depression, especially the religious context.

The Nineteenth-Century View

Religious melancholy was an especially important phenomenon among Protestant evangelicals. [Professor] J.H. Rubin suggested that the "system of theology and practice of piety [in early American Protestant culture] led to distinctly pathological consequences for believers who struggled to forge a life in precise conformity with these ultimate religious values." Given that one could never ultimately know God's plan, "doubt, despair, times of spiritual dryness, and 'dark nights of the soul' assailed believers." Escape from these episodes of despair through revival sermons and the revival itself became a social movement of awakening to a new light of religious enthusiasm that helped shape and drive the Protestant ethic and its resultant industry and productivity.

Twentieth-Century Ideas

By the beginning of the 20th century, however, religious melancholy was a phenomenon of the past. Pastoral care (which focused on moral management during the 19th century) had failed to cure religious melancholy. Freud expanded the psychoanalytic viewpoint to the community, even the religious community, despite his professed atheism. Religious experiences were no longer considered the cause of the more severe forms of mental illness. Conservative Protestants, by the mid-20th century, had rejoined the mainstream of American culture. Perhaps of most importance, the American religion of the 20th century emphasized the freedom of the individual. The sense of control and punishment by God, much less the control of a religious community, virtually disappeared.

Depression as a reaction to an act of God or the religious community therefore faded quickly, except for a few isolated examples. [Dr. Joseph] Eaton and [Robert] Weil performed an epidemiologic study among the Hutterites [Hutterites are an isolationist religious group, with qualities that are similar to the Amish and Mennonites] in northwestern North America at mid-20th century. This isolated group of religious pacifists valued simplicity, communal ownership of property, and government consensus, in marked contrast to the individualistic and increasingly secular lifestyle around them. Their social system was quite stable, yet the value of this stability was purchased at the cost of social conformity among its members. The protective social structure of the Hutterite community was associated with a high frequency of depression (both mild and severe) and feelings of guilt among those who feared that they might not live up to group expectations. On the other hand, character pathology was rare.

Religious melancholy, a reactive melancholy, flourished before the Enlightenment, persisted in many religious communities well into the 19th century, but virtually disappeared in the 20th century. Melancholy as a reaction did not die so quickly, for the theories of Freud were theories of a reactive depression. Even so, the biologic theme, as associated with the more severe depressions, gained new energy in Europe during the early 20th century, and 50 years later came to have a profound impact on late-20th-century American psychiatry.

Depression's Role in Bodily Disease

Marianne Szegedy-Maszak

Marianne Szegedy-Maszak, author of the following article, is a senior writer at U.S. News & World Report and a contributing writer for the Los Angeles Times. She discusses the recently discovered link between major depression and disease. Researchers have found, Szegedy-Maszak writes, that those who suffer from lifelong depression are more likely to be diagnosed with illnesses such as diabetes, heart disease, stroke, and even cancer. While doctors acknowledge that some of this may be due to depression sufferers not taking care of their bodies, they have also shown that the depression puts stress on the heart and arteries, as well as blood sugar, which can cause bodily illness. The link between depression and Alzheimer's disease is less solid, Szegedy-Maszak writes, but doctors suspect that depression sufferers may succumb to the disease faster.

Bryce Miller's work as an industrial engineer in Topeka, Kan., wasn't a whole lot more challenging than the job he faces in retirement: engineering his own medical care by 10 different doctors. Miller, 74, sees a team of specialists, which includes a cardiologist, a urologist and radiologist for prostate cancer, an endocrinologist for diabetes, a nephrologist for kidney problems, and a psychiatrist to manage the severe episodes of depression he has suffered during a long struggle with bipolar disorder. "I can't find a doctor who can handle all of it," he says.

It's impossible to pinpoint all the causes of Miller's illness; a combination of bad genes, bad luck, and bad diet probably gets much of the blame. But lately, he says, he's been wondering whether his mental state may have played a role, too. Medicine has recognized for some time that chronically sick people are prone to depression and that those affected have a tougher road back. Now, the signs are mounting that the spectrum of depressive illness, and perhaps even bitter loneliness, may actually make healthy people more vulnerable to a range of physical ailments. "There is a growing body of evidence suggesting that depression might be a causal risk factor in diseases like . . . heart disease, stroke, diabetes, and immune-based diseases like cancer and HIV/AIDS," says Dwight Evans, chair of psychiatry at the University of Pennsylvania medical school. "And there is also considerable recent evidence that mood disorders can affect the course of medical illnesses. It goes both ways. Depression may be both a cause and a consequence of medical illness."

Risk Factor

Consider a study published last month in the journal *Diabetologia*, which concluded that depressed adults have a 37 percent greater risk of developing type 2 diabetes than the rest of the population; other studies have suggested their risk actually doubles. (Apparently, English physician Thomas Willis was on to something when he wrote in 1674, "Diabetes is caused by melancholy.") One intriguing recent study of Alzheimer's patients revealed that those with a history of depression had more extensive plaques in their brains. Depressed postmenopausal women with no history of heart disease are much more likely to develop it and die of it than their peers. In March, University of Chicago researchers showed that loneliness can spike blood pressure by 30 points in older people. Pancreatic cancer, for reasons scientists don't understand, is often preceded by a serious depression before the disease asserts itself.

And when melancholy [depression] comes on the heels of disease, it appears to compound the physical insult. Diabetes is more likely to be uncontrolled, for example. And several studies have found that in the months right after a heart attack, the depressed patients are much more likely to die than the others.

If the researchers are right, the human cost of letting depression go untreated is staggering. Nearly 25 percent of American women and 10 percent of men will be clinically depressed at some point in their lives; a massive study conducted by the World Health Organization, Harvard University School of Public Health, and the World Bank found that by 2020, depression will be second only to heart disease as a cause of medical and physical disability. People who have suffered silently because their mental-health insurance benefits are so stingy got a glimmer of hope last week from the results of a large study showing that employers could beef up benefits without significantly raising costs.

What might explain the mind's influence on physical health? Certainly, chronic depression does not encourage a healthy lifestyle. "Depressed individuals don't exercise. They are more likely not to take medication, and it is harder for them to lose weight and stop smoking," says Nancy Frasure-Smith, a professor of psychiatry at the University of Montreal and McGill University who has long studied the link between depression and cardiovascular disease.

The Biochemistry

But depression also acts on the body's systems in ways scientists are only beginning to understand. Extra stress hormones are produced, for example—along with chemicals that trigger inflammation. When the hormone cortisol is secreted in response to stress, the body's blood glucose level rises to provide a burst of energy. A depressed brain's constant signal that it's under stress and needs more energy complicates the body's regulation of blood sugar. Might this explain why depression seems to both trigger and exacerbate diabetes?

A stress response may set depressed people up for cardiovascular disease, too—or aggravate it. When the blood-clotting system gets ready for impending injury, sticky cells called platelets go on high alert to slow down bleeding. In depressed people, one study showed, the platelets are more apt to be in this state of readiness. The problem: Clotting is what causes heart attacks and strokes. Chemicals called cytokines flood the bloodstream, as well. These messengers from the immune system cause inflammation, which makes blood vessels thicken and artery-hardening plaques form.

Researchers have also noted another stress reaction: The heart muscles of depressed patients lose flexibility. A normal heart transitions easily between its resting and beating states; more rigid muscle is less able to respond to the changing demands of the body for blood and oxygen. A study published last month in the *Journal of the American College of Cardiology* found that mental stress caused a more dramatic decrease in blood flow to the heart muscle—or ischemia—than a stress test on a treadmill. All told, stress and depression probably explain "close to 30 percent of the total risk of heart attacks," estimates David Sheps, professor of medicine and associate chief of cardiovascular medicine at the University of Florida.

It's way too soon to make the leap that depression is a direct cause of heart disease akin to smoking or high cholesterol, or that treatment—like quitting cigarettes—can reverse the damage or save lives. Indeed, two big recent studies have failed to show that heart patients live longer when they undergo therapy or take antidepressants. But medicine is intent upon dealing with the mental health of cardiac patients anyway, because people who are not depressed are more likely to lead heart-healthy lives; they exercise, take their medicines, lose weight, and stop smoking. "If you are a patient with heart disease, you need to know what your cholesterol level is, what your blood pressure is, and what diet and exercise program you will need to prevent a second heart attack. You should add to that list whether or not you are depressed," says Richard Stein, director of preventive cardiology at Beth Israel hospital in New York.

The majority of people who have survived some sort of heart event are, at least for a while. Some 65 percent of heart attack survivors are estimated to fall into depression, for example. According to Mended Hearts, the oldest and largest support group for people with heart disease, about 70 percent of patients who have gone through heart surgery, which often follows a heart attack, get depressed during the first year, and about a third continue to suffer from debilitating depression.

"I was just inside this ugly tunnel," says Dale Briggs, a Mended Hearts executive and an insurance fraud investigator from Fresno, Calif., who had a valve replaced in his heart 12 years ago at age 48 and was overwhelmed by the emotional consequences. He couldn't sleep, watched television for hours on end, and found it impossible to exercise or eat properly until his doctor prescribed medication and his depression lifted.

Brain Drain

The research linking depression to dementia is still in its infancy and has raised more questions than it has answered. One study published in February, by researchers at the University of Pittsburgh, found that adults with symptoms of depression scored a bit lower on cognitive tests than those who were not depressed, a finding that is consistent with extensive previous research on the way depression contributes to cognitive impairment. But only about 13 percent of the patients who eventually developed dementia were depressed.

At the same time, though, another group of researchers reported that the brains of Alzheimer's patients with a history of depression had more of the disease's characteristic tangles and plaques in the hippocampus—the area largely responsible for memory—than those of other patients. Moreover, their medical records indicated that they had succumbed more rapidly to the ravages of the illness. "About all we do know with certainty," says Michael Rapp, a resident at Mount Sinai medical school and one of the authors of the Alzheimer's study, "is that the biggest risk factor for Alzheimer's disease is old age."

What also seems certain, however mysterious all these connections may be, is that mental health can no longer be considered a separate issue. Realizing that there may be links between his mental and physical illness has brought Bryce Miller some peace with a body that has often confused him. "When they stuck my finger 15 years ago and found out that I was diabetic, it never occurred to me that my depression had something to do with it," he says. "But now it just seems so clear: The brain is always connected to the body."

Depression and Suicide

Joanne Kenen

In the following article, journalist Joanne Kenen describes Oregon senator Gordon Smith's efforts to pass a suicide-prevention bill after the suicide of his own son. The Smiths were a loving, close-knit family, Kenen writes, but despite their best efforts, their son Garrett fell into bouts of depression in his teens. Gordon and Sharon Smith tried to help their son by providing him with therapy, antidepressants, family time, and general love and support, but they were unable to stop him from hanging himself when he was twenty-one. Kenen writes that while Garrett showed many of the symptoms of suicidal behavior, he was not hospitalized by his therapists. The Smiths however, have found comfort in their efforts to prevent suicide in other depressed people. Gordon Smith's bill increases funding for suicide awareness and public education, while his wife has become a public speaker and mental-health advocate. Joanne Kenen is a Washington correspondent for the Reuters news agency.

The Senate chamber was largely empty when Gordon Smith took the floor to introduce a bill. But when the Oregon Republican started to cry, colleagues rushed to the floor and gathered around him.

It had been ten months since Garrett Lee Smith, the second of Smith's three children, placed his beloved bulldog, Ollie, in a kennel in the kitchen with extra food and water, dimmed the lights in his apartment, turned on soft music, and knelt to die alone in a closet the day before his 22nd birthday. The Garrett Lee Smith Memorial Act, a suicide-prevention bill, was his father's way of saying goodbye.

Smith's speech was raw. He recalled the first time he met Garrett, who like the Smiths' other two children was adopted

Joanne Kenen, "To Save Someone Else's Son," *Washingtonian*, July 2005. Copyright © 2005 Washington Magazine, Inc. Reproduced by permission of the author.

as a baby. He related his pride at discovering Garrett's high IQ—and then the ache at finding out about his son's learning disabilities. He described how Garrett, in his teens and twenties, had experienced episodes of depression that "filled his spirit with hopelessness and clouded his future in darkness. He saw only despair ahead and felt only pain in the present, pain and despair so potent that he saw suicide as a refuge, a release."

The response from fellow senators was as dramatic as the speech. Harry Reid, soon to become the Senate Democratic leader, rose. Reid, a soft-spoken Nevadan, is not given to emotional excess. He spoke about how he and his wife, Landra, had flown to Oregon to attend Garrett's funeral: "We were so impressed because no one—no one—tried to mask what happened to Garrett Smith."

Reid said that when his father, a miner, shot himself to death in 1972, the family did not discuss it publicly for years; they had trouble coming to terms with it even in private. Eventually they came to understand that he had probably been depressed his whole life. Reid wondered if a prevention program, had one existed when his father was young, could have saved him.

Then Don Nickles, an Oklahoma Republican known for his conservatism—and not necessarily the compassionate kind—stood up to say that his dad, too, had taken his life. "I am not going to go into the details," he said, "but it is a lot of pain." Nickles, who has since retired from the Senate, pledged to support the bill, saying it would save more lives than they would ever know. Then he sat down.

Some fellow senators who had known Nickles for years say they had not known about his father's suicide. Gordon and Sharon Smith didn't know until Garrett died and Don and Linda Nickles were the first to show up at their front door.

Pete Domenici, a crusty New Mexico Republican, had gone home early that July day. But when he saw Smith, then Reid and Nickles, pouring their hearts out on C-SPAN, he put on a suit and rushed back to the Senate. Domenici has a schizophrenic daughter and has long championed better insurance for mental health.

Smith's bill passed the Senate unanimously that day.

Funds to Prevent Suicide

Garrett's death was a turning point not only in the personal lives of Gordon and Sharon Smith but also in the political life of a senator whose moderate path has surprised those who thought the former frozen-food mogul in well-tailored suits would be a predictable conservative.

Sharon was a stay-at-home mom not comfortable in the public eye. Since Garrett's death, she has made speeches and become active with mental-health advocacy groups. "Whoever thought this is what we'd be known for?" she says. The Smiths are now driven to save someone else's child—even if with all their money, connections, and efforts, they were unable to save their own.

The Garrett Lee Smith Memorial Act is a modest bill. But not much got passed [in 2004], not even modest bills, and Smith knows he has at least made a down payment on a suicide-prevention strategy.

"These are the first federal dollars that will find their way to governments and states trying to prevent suicides," says Jerry Reed, director of the Suicide Prevention Action Network, known as SPAN USA.

The law sets up a national suicide center that will gather and evaluate data to help figure out what works and what doesn't. It gives states grants to develop youth suicide screening as well as early intervention and prevention programs.

The programs target kids in schools, mental-health and substance-abuse programs, the juvenile-justice system, and foster care. The law also has a campus-based component aimed at reaching college students—kids like Garrett who leave home for the first time and fray at the emotional seams.

Surveys by the American College Health Association and other groups have found that more college students are experiencing severe depression and other emotional challenges. Suicide is the third leading cause of death for Americans ages 10 to 24.

Although Smith's bill passed the Senate, it took two months to get it through the House. Some conservatives didn't think mental health was the government's concern. Others objected to the price tag, up to $82 million over three years. Congress would end up appropriating $11.5 million for the first year, not the $15 million Smith sought.

After some prodding and dealing—and the inclusion of stricter parental-consent rules for adolescent screening—the bill passed the House by a large margin and returned to the Senate for final passage on September 9, 2004, which would have been Garrett's 23rd birthday. President [George W.] Bush signed it in October in a private ceremony. The Smiths and their other two children, Brittany, now 25, and Morgan, 16, attended.

"It was the hardest thing I've ever done politically and the best thing I've ever done legislatively," Gordon Smith says. "Whatever culpability I have in Garrett's death, we can add meaning to his life."

Struggling to Understand

College sweethearts, Sharon and Gordon Smith were married five years before infant Brittany came into their lives. Enchanted by parenthood, they applied to adopt another child, expecting to wait a few years. Brittany was only 20 months old when the phone rang with news of a little boy. The Smiths took off so quickly for Spokane that they left a note on their door for Sharon's parents, who were on their way to visit: "Make yourself at home, we've gone to get you a new baby grandchild."

Garrett was "a beautiful child," his father says. The montage of photos on his funeral program shows an all-American kid, whether he's a toddler playing in the sand or a teenager in a football jersey. He's smiling in all the pictures. He looks happy. "Everyone loved him," says his mom. "He was a darling boy."

Intellectually, Gordon and Sharon Smith now understand that depression—and it's not clear whether Garrett was suffering severe clinical depression or had developed bipolar disorder—is an illness, like leukemia or diabetes. But as they talk about Garrett, they still seem to be searching for something they missed, for something that would help them make sense out of what in their hearts they do not seem able to comprehend.

"When you lose a child in suicide, the first instinct is self-recrimination," his father says.

As they recall sweet things about their son, they keep second-guessing themselves, wondering aloud, seeking reassurance, searching for absolution.

When Garrett was little, he sometimes banged his head as he tried to fall asleep—but the pediatrician reassured them it was not uncommon. His speech came in a little slow—but the speech experts said not to worry, it was still normal. In third grade, dyslexia was diagnosed, but he had the brains and determination to compensate. The family moved twice, once when Gordon joined the state legislature—Garrett was in sixth grade—and again a few years later when he entered the Senate, but Garrett seemed to adjust. Teachers and counselors and learning specialists often commented that he was such a well-adjusted child.

Adolescent Troubles

And he had a lot going for him. He was an athlete. He was popular. He was an Eagle Scout. He shared his family's Mormon faith. He had close friends he kept from early childhood to the end of his life. He had a caring family and supportive teachers, coaches, and scoutmasters. He was an easy kid, an obedient kid, even into his teens. He was honest with his parents and shared a lot with them. Except the sadness.

As a teenager, he began to experience mood swings. "It would be like somebody hitting a switch, and he wasn't functioning for a while," his father says. The first crisis came when he was a junior in high school. Garrett was drinking, which isn't just against the law for a teenager; it's against the Mormon faith. He was drinking in secret, and it scared him enough to come to his parents for help.

The Smiths recognized the alcohol abuse as a mental-health problem, not a moral failing or adolescent rebellion, and they sought help. The doctor suggested they enroll Garrett in a twice-weekly teen substance-abuse program. Garrett attended faithfully. The Smiths were given tools for monitoring him.

The doctor mentioned that Garrett had an "addictive personality" and was "self-medicating," but he didn't help the Smiths understand what that meant, didn't suggest that prescription medication might be in order, didn't help them connect the dots. "Nobody ever said to me," Sharon says, "that he's self-medicating because he's depressed."

Garrett's parents did worry about the stress of life in Washington and at his competitive private school, Bullis, in Potomac. Brittany had finished high school, but Sharon packed up the two boys and went home to Oregon so Garrett could complete his senior year at Pendleton High School. The Smiths kept their house in Bethesda; Gordon flew home every weekend.

Garrett liked being back with his childhood friends. He stayed sober and got his diploma. He prepared for his next goal, a two-year mission for the Church of Jesus Christ of Latter-day Saints that would take him to England. Filling out a health history for the mission, Garrett checked off "yes" when asked about depression. "That is the first time we saw the word 'depression,'" Gordon says.

"I remember how shocked you were," Sharon adds.

They offered Garrett medical help, but he declined, saying the depression wasn't that bad. "I think I'll be okay," he told his mom and dad. "I just wanted to be honest."

They worried, but they knew that Garrett would be with friends and that the mission leader, who had experience dealing with young adults, would keep an eye on their son. Garrett sometimes spoke about struggling with his emotions, but he showed up for work every day for two years.

Worries About the Future

Garrett returned home and in early 2003 enrolled at Utah Valley State College, at the base of the Wasatch Mountains. With a mix of vocational training and low-key liberal arts, it was a place where a smart young man who didn't read very well could find a niche. "It was a good match for him," Gordon says. Garrett, who dreamed of owning a restaurant, entered a culinary-arts program.

He shared an apartment with several young men, including Ethan, a childhood friend. School wasn't easy for Garrett; he often relied on recorded books but did okay.

There were danger signs. He was drinking again, and his friends learned of at least one incident with pills. He slept too much, yet he asked his mother to get him sleeping pills. She refused. He cut his upper arm, apparently intentionally, although his parents did not learn of that until later. Little annoyances, like a scratch on a car, became huge problems.

He sometimes expressed hopelessness about his future. When those moods struck, and they struck more frequently that spring and summer, he was beyond his parents' reach—"beyond reason, beyond rationality," his father says.

Ethan made Garrett call home that winter. "I think I'm ready to get some medicine," he told his parents. They helped get him a prescription for an antidepressant. Ethan stayed in touch with the Smiths, and he and others in a circle of friends watched out for Garrett, persuading him to hand over his hunting rifle and target gun for safekeeping.

When the semester ended, Garrett's two best friends left for New York for the summer. Garrett stayed behind, living alone and working a telephone survey job. From afar, his parents knew his despondency was deepening.

That May, they got him to start seeing a psychologist twice a week, and they kept sending him his medication. Because Garrett was an adult, his parents and the therapist had legal and moral obligations to respect his privacy, but they shared some things. Sharon was always comforted when the bill showed up in her mailbox, confirmation that her boy was getting help.

In July they went to Utah to check on Garrett and saw he wasn't taking care of himself. He had put on weight. He was disheveled.

"What would make you happy?" his parents asked.

"Take me back to England," he said.

Mixed Signs

The Senate's August recess was coming, and the Smiths changed their plans. Garrett spent a week with his parents in Washington, visiting old high-school friends. Then the three of them went to England for two weeks. He was mostly fine, except for the three times he curled up in the back seat of the car, almost fetally, and said, "I'm not feeling very good."

Looking back, they are glad they took that trip. It gave them some happy memories. It gave Garrett, they realized later, a chance to say goodbye to friends, a chance to say goodbye to them.

He returned to Utah for the fall semester. Sharon and Gordon were more afraid than ever: Garrett had told them on the last night of their vacation that he sometimes feared he would take his life. Sharon and Gordon considered all sorts of options, including hospitalization, but Garrett resisted that idea so vehemently that his parents feared it could be counterproductive and that he would talk himself out of any hospital in 24 hours.

Instead, they made Garrett see a psychiatrist, as well as his psychologist, as soon as he got back to school. The doctor who evaluated Garrett changed his medication but later told the family he hadn't appeared suicidal.

The family was relieved by signs that Garrett might be coming out of it. His friends were back; classes resumed. He was enjoying his red BMW—they had splurged when they bought him what they vowed would be the only car they would ever give him. They sent him Ollie, the family's English bulldog, for company.

Even the week of his death, there were positive signs. Garrett went out on Friday night for dinner with seven friends. He ran into another pal at the video-rental outlet and made a plan to get together the following week. He opened the box of birthday presents Sharon sent when it arrived on Saturday, not waiting until Tuesday.

And then on Sunday night, he entered that closet.

Aftermath of a Suicide

As best as the Smiths can reconstruct, Garrett took care of the dog, ordered a pizza, and wrote them a note on his computer—not necessarily in that order. He took pills and drank whiskey and put a noose around his neck as he knelt in his closet. When he passed out from the drugs and alcohol, the noose tightened. "He did it gently," his mother hopes. "Garrett was gentle."

A friend, worried that Garrett had not been in class, came by the apartment Monday afternoon. The door was unlocked and he let himself in. He heard Ollie whining in the kitchen and released him from the kennel. The friend followed the agitated dog to the bedroom, to the closet, to Garrett.

Parts of the suicide note that the Smiths have made public are sad: "Put me in the ground and forget about me."

And parts are kind. "If it is any consolation," he wrote his parents, "your love is the only thing in my life I know will never change. I'd simply like to feel the same about myself. I love you so much. And just think your son won't feel that every day pain anymore.

"I just wish I could love myself as you love me."

Later that evening Montgomery County police knocked on the Smiths' door, and the senator went into action. "We never thought of hiding what happened," Smith says. He handwrote a press release and began planning a memorial service. He started designing the gravesite. The pedestal, his wife says, was rough-hewn to show Garrett's unfinished life.

Though not intended as political advocacy, their forthrightness had impact. The dean of students at the University of Oregon later told the senator that after the family announcement, the campus health center was flooded with students reaching out for help.

About 5,000 people attended the funeral in Pendleton, a town of fewer than 20,000. Six senators made the trip. Others, like Nickles and Ted Kennedy, gave emotional support back in Washington.

"Underlying the lion's roar," Smith once marveled of Kennedy, "he has a heart that is filled with compassion."

Turning to Legislation

It was Mike DeWine who handed Smith a legislative lifeline. An Ohio Republican, DeWine lost one of his daughters in a car accident nearly 12 years ago. He'd been working with two Democrats—Christopher Dodd of Connecticut and Jack Reed of Rhode Island—on two youth-suicide initiatives; Dodd's focused on teens and Reed's on the college group. But it was

2004, a presidential election year, and not much was getting through Congress, especially not feel-good legislation with mostly Democratic support.

Now DeWine, chair of one of the Senate health subcommittees, knew how to give the bill a push—and maybe give one of his Senate friends a bit of renewed purpose.

"I asked him if he wanted to testify. I wasn't sure if he'd be ready. It had only been a few months," DeWine recalls. Smith agreed, and he wrote out his testimony in longhand on a legal pad.

With Sharon by his side in the committee room, he read it carefully, moving some in the audience to tears. From then on, he worked hard for passage.

Sharon Smith, whose life has revolved around family and church far more than around politics, has found herself in demand as a speaker. Oregon's Democratic governor appointed her to the state task force on mental health. She joined the boards of SPAN USA and TeenScreen, a Columbia University program that helps detect depression in young people. The Smiths endowed a TeenScreen program at St. Anthony Hospital in Pendleton, to offer voluntary mental-health checkups to middle-schoolers. They established a memorial library and Web site through St. Anthony, making mental-health resources more available to the community.

The Web site includes excerpts of some of the more than 10,000 letters the family has received since Garrett's death. Some describe how someone can seem so normal on the outside and suffer so deeply within. That normalcy is part of Sharon's message. "We've learned that mentally ill people can behave very normally," she says. "It's not the crazy person of someone's imagination."

She gives speeches or attends events about twice in a typical month; she still has one teenager at home. Speechmaking does not come easily to her: "It's really emotional when you have to share this."

People walk up to her all the time now, survivors sharing stories of loved ones lost to suicide, parents of depressed teens sharing their fears. "There's not a day that goes by that someone doesn't approach me," she says. "I can make a difference. I can comfort them. I can tell them not to be ashamed and embarrassed if a loved one has a mental-health issue."

In her wallet she carries a card listing warning signs of suicide, signs she wishes she had known two years ago. They include having trouble sleeping or eating, risk-taking, behavior changes, drug and alcohol use, giving away prized possessions, being preoccupied with death. Garrett had many of these.

Not Parents' Fault

She stays in touch with Garrett's friends, telling them that they were wonderful to Garrett and that his problems were not their fault. Every few months, she drops a note to a "sweet little girl" who broke a date with Garrett the day before he walked into the closet; the young woman was unsure if she was ready for a new boyfriend so soon after her last breakup. Sharon worries about that girl.

Sharon knows that people hear of a suicide and assume that the parenting was somehow defective. She doesn't believe that. But she feels sorry for parents who were estranged from a suicidal child and for families that had argued with a child, maybe about homework or a dent in the family car, who later took his or her life. She knows that even with all this pain, she has much for which to be grateful.

"I was a good mom. I was able to do everything for Garrett," she says. When a friend cleaned out Garrett's apartment—something she could not bring herself to do—he found dozens of cards and notes Sharon had written Garrett in his months away from home. "He had kept every one."

Gordon seems more torn. "I've always been a driven person, both in business and politics," he says. "I know my children had the best mother in the world. That gave me the professional elbow room. But when I was home, I think I was a good daddy."

Sharon, and Smith's own staff, saw a change in him, a measure of peace, when his bill was enacted. "The bill was his way of being able to shut a door, to be able to say, 'We've done this, son,'" Sharon says.

Senator Smith is still working on more funding for suicide prevention, and he's pushing to preserve a federal safety net to help the impoverished mentally ill. He can find purpose again, he says, in public life and more peace in his memories.

"We take solace in the time we had with Garrett," he told the Senate that July day. "And say to all those who suffer the loss of love ones that the very best antidote for grief is the gratitude you had for your loved one for a time on Earth."

Understanding Postpartum Depression

Mark Levy and Stacy Sabraw

Mark Levy is a professor of psychiatry at the University of California in San Francisco. Stacy Sabraw is a New York-based freelance journalist. In the follow article, Levy and Sabraw describe the symptoms and effects of postpartum depression and the rarer but much more dangerous postpartum psychosis. A majority of women experience some sort of sad or mild depressed feelings soon after having a baby, the two authors write, but a percentage develop postpartum depression, which is a diagnosable illness like clinical depression. A few of those will develop postpartum psychosis, which is a mental illness that can require hospitalization to prevent the mother from harming herself or her baby. Many factors can affect whether a woman develops postpartum depression, Levy and Sabraw write, including whether she was depressed before her pregnancy, her social support system, and the trauma of her labor and delivery.

Postpartum mood disorders are more common than we realize: Up to 80 percent of new mothers experience mild depression within a year of giving birth. If the "baby blues" persist, depression can escalate to dangerous levels, influencing some women to experience psychosis and—in rare and tragic cases—to kill their offspring.

During the first six weeks after giving birth, Jennifer Moyer was grateful for her beautiful new son and supportive husband. Yet she wasn't herself. She felt somewhat irritable and was having difficulty sleeping. And just after her first postpartum physical checkup, things began to unravel—and fast. The feeling that some unnamed harm was coming to her son over-

Mark Levy and Stacy Sabraw, "Moms Who Kill," *Psychology Today*, vol. 35, December 2002. Reproduced by permission.

whelmed her; she became hyperprotective, not allowing any-one—even her husband—to hold the baby. One month later, after three sleepless nights, anxiety and fear consumed her to a point where her son had to be physically removed from her, and she was forcibly taken to the hospital. Moyer was in the throes of postpartum psychosis.

The focus of a lot of media attention, this illness gained a voice largely due to the story of Andrea Yates, the woman found guilty of drowning her five children in a bathtub in Texas [in 2001]. Yates, who has a long history of mental ill-ness, confessed to jurors that Satan had ordered her to kill her children. Though diagnosed with postpartum psychosis, she was judged capable of discerning right from wrong and sen-tenced to life in prison. Despite considerable research into the nature of postpartum mood disorders, there is still no clear medical consensus on what causes it and how it should be treated. "Having grown up expecting motherhood to be one of the best times of life, many women suffer alone, feeling miserable but unaware that postpartum mood disorders have a name," explains Karen Kleiman, M.S.W., founder and direc-tor of the Postpartum Stress Center in Philadelphia.

Discerning Symptoms

As many as 50 to 80 percent of women experience some de-gree of emotional "letdown" following childbirth—the so-called "baby blues." Fortunately, its more extreme sister disor-der, postpartum psychosis, is rare, affecting only about one in 1,000 new mothers.

The baby blues, though, are common for numerous rea-sons. The baby's crying and the mother's interrupted sleep and soreness from breast-feeding are enough to make any woman feel irritable, if not overwhelmed and tearful. These feelings typically begin three to four days after the baby is born, according to Kleiman, but normally dissipate on their own within a few weeks.

If the blues last for more than two weeks, however, the new mother may be suffering from a condition of intermediate severity, postpartum depression (PPD), a mood disorder on par with clinical depression. Twelve to 16 percent of women experience PPD, which results in feelings of despondency, inadequacy as a mother, impaired concentration or memory and/or loss of interest or pleasure in activities.

Some women, like Moyer, also become paralyzed with fear and concern for the baby's safety. If such symptoms appear, it is important to seek professional consultation to help differentiate PPD from other conditions such as obsessive-compulsive disorder. Symptoms of anxiety are frequently an aspect of clinical depression, but true obsessive-compulsive symptoms signify a different disorder that needs proper diagnosis and treatment.

Shoshana Bennett, Ph.D., a special-education teacher, began suffering from these types of anxious feelings almost immediately after giving birth. "I felt helpless and hopeless," Bennett says now. "I was so afraid someone was going to hurt my baby that every day after my husband went to work, I would place all movable furniture behind the front door."

Though debilitating, the emotional reactions to being a new mom that signify depression are not as severe as those associated with postpartum psychosis, of which the predominant symptom is a "break" with reality—a loss of the ability to discern what is real from what is not. For instance, a woman with PPD may experience violent thoughts about her baby but recognizes that those thoughts are wrong and potentially dangerous. In that case, she will not act on them.

Psychotic Beliefs

A woman with full-fledged psychosis, however, has temporarily lost the judgment needed to make this assessment. Very often, a woman with psychosis experiences a frightening sense of merging—she can't differentiate between where she ends and where her baby begins. Psychotic merger is so terrifying that she may try to avoid losing her sense of self by either committing suicide or infanticide, also known as suicide by proxy.

This was the case with Andrea Yates, whose suicide attempts ended with the deliberate drowning of her children. Perhaps, in her mind, to prevent the "loss of self," she was compelled to kill her children or herself, or both.

Infanticide is a very rare phenomenon; only about 4 percent of women who become psychotic kill their babies. Perhaps even fewer tragedies would occur if proper education and treatment were more readily available.

Researchers who study infanticide distinguish several different groups of parents who murder their offspring. Some kill as a result of psychotic delusions—the dread of parent-child merger or the belief that the child is trying to harm or kill them. Others murder their children out of profound depression and hopelessness. Often they carry strong religious ideas that killing their child will enable them both to enter an afterlife more peaceful than their current life. Susan Smith, the South Carolina mother who attempted to drown herself and her children by driving her automobile into a lake, may be an example of someone in this group, although Smith ended up killing her children but not herself.

Tragically, there are also parents who kill their children out of vengeance and rage against the other parent. They want to hurt the other parent by depriving them of their most cherished relationship. This type of infanticide is committed far more frequently by fathers.

Assessing the Source

As with most mental illnesses, what causes the onset of postpartum mood disorders is still a matter of research and debate. Much of the medical community believes these syndromes may be caused by chemical imbalances in the brain—

specifically shifts in hormone levels. According to Postpartum Support International (PSI), a network of mental health professionals and others concerned with promoting postpartum mental health and social support, the most well-researched theory to date suggests that a sharp drop in estrogen and progesterone following delivery is the culprit.

Research currently under way at the National Institute of Mental Health is examining these hormone-mediated mood shifts. And Victor Pop, Ph.D., of the University of Tilburg in the Netherlands, presented his own findings at the annual meeting of London's Royal College of Psychiatrists, suggesting that women who produce certain thyroid antibodies during pregnancy were nearly three times more likely to experience depression after childbirth.

"I think there will be a role for hormones in treating postpartum illnesses in the future," says Valerie Raskin, M.D., clinical associate professor at the University of Chicago. "[Hormones] will probably be used as a treatment first, then later as a preventive measure. The reproductive process may be the kindling, and the drop in hormones after childbirth may be the ember that starts the fire."

Various nonhormonal factors may also contribute to postpartum disorders of mood. Some studies suggest a relationship between a traumatic obstetric experience and PPD. Women who had caesarean deliveries, for instance, were significantly more susceptible to mood disorders as noted in one study appearing in the *Australian and New Zealand Journal of Psychiatry.*

Thyroid disease may also be a physiological trigger, suggests research by Stephen Pariser, M.D., a psychiatrist and mood-disorders specialist at Ohio State University Medical Center. Women's thyroid levels drop significantly after giving birth, and low thyroid levels have long been associated with depression-like symptoms. Having a personal or family history of mood disorders also increases the odds of developing PPD, pointing to a possible genetic factor.

Personal and Societal Pressures

Women who develop PPD or postpartum psychosis following delivery have a significantly greater risk of developing these conditions after subsequent childbirth. These women should be counseled about future pregnancies. If they do conceive additional children, careful psychiatric monitoring is mandatory.

Certainly, social elements also play an integral role in postpartum well-being. One important factor is a lack of social support, which includes poor relationships with others and insufficient childcare during the pre- and postnatal period. Strong support systems can help nurture and maintain self-esteem at stressful times, Kleiman asserts. "In turn, high levels of self esteem are linked with adaptive coping behaviors—feeling entitled to ask for help, for example."

As a society, we tend to romanticize motherhood, creating a disparity between a woman's expectations and the reality that she will experience. "Society reinforces the myth of the perfect baby in the arms of the perfect mother, with all her maternal instincts intact," says Kleiman. "When there is a significant discrepancy between what a woman anticipates and what she actually experiences, guilt, confusion and great unhappiness can result."

In addition to societal pressures, personal adversities such as loss of a loved one, marital conflict or lack of financial security, can put some women at greater risk, according to PSI. Lifestyle and role changes also create internal conflict and stress: A new mother may lose the independence, spontaneity, personal time, sleep and physical shape that she once had, along with her role as an attention-drawing pregnant woman or as a career woman. Finally, she may simply miss adult company in general. "Women with PPD will find adapting to these losses especially difficult," Kleiman notes, "because of their increased vulnerability."

Options for Treatment

Most experts agree that combining talk therapy with medication seems the most successful approach to treating PPD. "Medication is warranted," Raskin explains, "because the situation is urgent and the quickest treatment makes sense." Depending upon the patient, psychotherapy may be combined with both group support and medication, which is prescribed according to the patient's individual symptoms while monitoring the various drugs' side effects.

The most commonly prescribed are the newer antidepressants, including Prozac, Zoloft, Paxil, Celexa, Wellbutrin, Serzone and Effexor, as well as antianxiety drugs such as Ativan, Lorazepam and Klonopin. When the underlying cause of PPD is bipolar affective disorder, mood stabilizers—Lithium or Depakote, for instance—are also appropriate.

For women experiencing postpartum psychosis, more aggressive treatment is required. These mothers may be a threat to both themselves and their babies. Psychiatric hospitalization, as well as antipsychotic and other psychiatric medications, is standard treatment along with individual, group or cognitive behavioral psychotherapy.

And because at least half of women with PPD experience a recurrence of the illness after having another child, responsible parenting necessitates careful thought and medical planning before deciding to get pregnant again. Once PPD is present, "all resources must go toward treating the mother," advises Raskin. "Stress of any sort, including the stress of caring for children, will prevent the mother from healing."

Effective prevention would help render treatment less necessary, avert emotional damage to children and potentially save lives. Shoshana Bennett is one mother who might have benefited from preventive measures. Instead, her childbirth classes concentrated on breathing techniques and what to pack for the hospital. And during her first postpartum checkup, Bennett's obstetrician glossed over her weight gain of 40 pounds and uncontrollable weepiness.

When Bennett mentioned to her family that she was having a difficult time, her mother-in-law—a postpartum nurse for 20 years—told Bennett's husband, "Shoshana is a mother now. She needs to stop complaining and just do it." Bennett's own mother was supportive but, despite her background in therapy, failed to recognize the signs of serious emotional illness. Bennett also began seeing a psychologist, who only probed for issues in her past. Eventually, about two years after the birth of each of her two children, Bennett's obsessive concerns finally faded on their own.

Several years later, Bennett happened to see a television program on postpartum depression. "I cried for an hour, looked at my husband and said, 'That's me!'" she says. Afterward, she earned her Ph.D. in clinical psychology and founded a self-help group for postpartum disorder sufferers. Then in 1992, she was named president of the Postpartum Health Alliance, a California state organization.

Support of Medical Community

Today, the discussion of postpartum mood disorders is often inadequate in reference manuals. General physicians can find the terms postnatal depression, postpartum depression and puerperal psychosis in the *International Classification of Diseases* manual, says Cheryl Meyer, Ph.D., J.D., an associate psychology professor at Wright State University in Dayton, Ohio. "However, they may only use these diagnoses for patients whose symptoms do not meet criteria for other disorders, such as depression," she explains.

Jennifer Moyer, now a coordinator for PSI and a postpartum support consultant, understands firsthand why medical professionals need to pay more attention to postpartum mood disorders. For her, recovery came after two years of medication, therapy and family support, and she believes that talking to someone who has experienced a severe postpartum mood disorder firsthand is essential for recovery. She now combines her own experience with her background in health care marketing to advocate for education and prenatal and postnatal screening.

Until the health insurance industry and government agencies are willing to allocate sufficient resources to guarantee the presence of skilled psychiatrists and psychologists on pre- and postnatal-care teams, assessing and treating postpartum mood disorders will continue to fall through the cracks. Both Moyer and Bennett join other health care professionals in the hope that efforts to focus on women's emotional needs before and after pregnancy will gain momentum. This effort will help other women and their families avoid disabling yet treatable illnesses or, tragically, from having to endure another preventable murder of an innocent infant.

CHAPTER 2

Personal Perspectives on Depression

Motherhood and Depression

Kathryn Harrison

Kathryn Harrison is a novelist and essayist who has also written two memoirs about her childhood and mental health problems. In the following excerpt from her memoir The Mother Knot, *Harrison recounts her struggle with depression and anxiety after weaning her third child. The loss of the bond, she writes, spurred a severe bout with the illness from which she had suffered for many years previously. The help of her therapist and antidepressants, Harrison writes, alleviated her symptoms to an extent but lingering problems with her relationship with her mother lay at the root of the problem.*

There's still a bottle of milk in our freezer, six ounces expressed from my breasts and poured into a sterilized container to have on hand should our daughter get hungry when I'm not home. There used to be more frozen bottles, as many as a dozen, but our daughter is three now; she hasn't nursed for almost a year. The single bottle hidden among the foil-wrapped leftovers and cartons of ice cream is one I saved for myself—a benign little keepsake, or so I thought at the time, unable to imagine that the apparently sentimental souvenir would be revealed as a dark, even perverse, fetish.

The daughter for whom I froze my milk is our third child. After she was born I had a tubal ligation. I nursed her longer than I did her older sister and brother because I knew I wouldn't be returning to this one thing I did so well, so happily. Never again, under any other circumstances, would I be able to answer a loved one's desire so completely. My daughter passed one after another milestone of babyhood—she walked, talked, used her full set of teeth to eat whatever she wanted— and still I postponed the separation of weaning.

By May 2002 my youngest child was twenty-six months old and lifted my shirt only at bedtime or when she needed reassurance, comfort that was hers whether she nursed or not. At the end of that month I used a business trip to help me accomplish what I'd avoided as long as I was near her. All day and all night for a week I wore a tight sports bra, the effect of which was to bind my aching breasts and suppress the production of milk. When I showered my chest throbbed and my nipples leaked. For a few days they did. Then the body began to understand; the swelling diminished.

Onset of Depression

Back home, despite a sudden June heat wave, I wore high-necked shirts and tucked them into my waistband. When my daughter asked to nurse, fondling me through the fabric, I told her how proud I was to have such a wonderful big girl, and together we listed the differences between big girls and babies, who drink from their mothers and can't have apple juice or chocolate milk in a cup. A secure and cheerful child, my daughter adapted quickly. I however, suffered a plunge in mood and waited for what didn't happen: to feel better, or at least less bereft.

Summer became a season of compulsive work and little else. Diversions I'd enjoyed in the past—trips to the beach, dinner parties, movies, tennis—were leached of pleasure, colorless, tedious, exhausting. Everything required more energy than I had, especially pretending that I wasn't depressed. Sleep was elusive, and I began, on those nights I was awake hours after turning off the light, to sneak a half milligram of stale Xanax.

The tranquilizer had been prescribed four years earlier, when I'd suffered a depression serious enough that, once hospitalized, I found a metal mirror in my bathroom, not a glass one I could break and use against myself. The admitting nurse searched my overnight bag and confiscated my disposable razor; she told me that there were no circumstances under which I was permitted to close my door and that if I wanted to shave my legs or armpits I could do so only with supervision. But all I wanted was nightfall, the eight o'clock distribution of pills that hastened the patients to sleep, silencing the hallways.

Xanax was valuable; I'd never considered discarding the fifty or so that remained after I recovered. I still had enough that for weeks I could avoid acknowledging the anxiety and insomnia that had characterized the onset of my previous breakdown. Soon it would be September, I told myself, the month I'd always loved best, the one that, when I was a child, had rescued me from a long season spent with my family, and offered then what I thought it would now: the solace of routine.

A Child in Pain

Our older daughter, twelve, and our son, ten, began school immediately after Labor Day. One week passed, then another. I was still waiting for a discernible lift in my spirits when, on Tuesday, September 24, our son fell ill. Although he'd never before had respiratory problems—at least not any of which we'd been aware—he was stricken with a severe asthma attack and spent five days in the hospital, three of them in pediatric ICU. Day after night after day I sat beside his bed, trying not to watch the monitor that displayed the jagged peaks and troughs of his elevated heart rate, the immediate fall in the level of oxygen in his blood when I removed his mask for a moment to untangle a snarl of tubes pulling on his IV. Treated every other hour with albuterol, a bronchodilator with stimulant side effects, my child slept little but drifted in and out of half-waking nightmares. Under the spell of one of these he screamed out in terror, and when I approached to reassure him, he didn't recognize me, he screamed louder.

What had he seen that frightened him? I asked myself. What kind of monster?

Past Memories

By now I'd fallen prey to the sinister associations that can attend deepening depression. Did this explain why I failed to distinguish one oxygen mask from another? The piece of molded plastic that fit over my son's nose and mouth summoned a mask I'd seen before, another clear green one I'd adjusted just as I did his. My mother had used it to breathe when she was dying of breast cancer, choking on it, her lungs filled with metastases, her hospital bed ensnared in a similar thicket of monitors and coils of tubing, gleaming metal gas cocks poking through the wall, a bag of blood hanging from a hook.

The chime of an IV pump, the hiss of oxygen, the unanswered telephones and endless paging of doctors, the broadcast blips of beating hearts: an electronic clamor muffled present groans and cries and returned me to my mother's bedside, to her tubes and her wires and her suffering—and to my panic at losing her before we could manage a reconciliation or even an honest farewell.

Before my son's illness, I'd congratulated myself for reaching a kind of acceptance of my tortured relationship with my mother. I'd been her only child, the baby she wasn't prepared to raise, the daughter she gave to her parents. I was the girl who loved and hated her mother in equal measure, whose longing was obvious and whose rage had always been concealed, even—especially—from herself. But I'd thought all that was behind me. I'd even told my analyst I was quitting therapy because I was increasingly bored by what had once compelled me: hashing and rehashing past agonies. . . .

An Attack of Rage

On a Sunday when my husband was out of town and my older daughter was at a friend's house, the sliding door to my son's bedroom got stuck. I couldn't close it. This had happened before; all that was required to fix the door was gently rocking it back onto its track. But I couldn't do it this time. I lacked forbearance, balance. When I'm nervous I'm clumsy. I lose touch with my body and mismanage spatial relationships.

There was a hammer on the shelf, and I used it to tap the door, top and bottom, but I couldn't budge it. Immediately I flew into a raging tantrum, hurled myself at the door, pulled on the old glass knob, pounded and cursed. It was only when I struck the knob so hard that it broke, gashing my middle finger, that I stopped, gratified by the sight of my blood, gratified and calmed. *Good*, I thought, watching it run down my wrist. *Bleed*, I thought.

My son and younger daughter stared at me from the adjoining room, silent and amazed. I had never before behaved like this in front of them, or anyone. "Sorry," I said. "I'm really sorry. Mom's stressed-out. Stressed-out, that's all."

"About what?" my son asked carefully. He knew—he must have known, for he knows me through and through—that the answer was at least in part him, the asthma.

"Work," I lied. "I'm behind. I missed a deadline."

Downstairs, I sat on the bathroom floor and watched the cut saturate a wad of tissues. I pulled back the flap of skin to assess its depth. Already I understood my paroxysm: the door was stuck so I couldn't close it; I couldn't seal off my son's room and run the HEPA filter; I couldn't make sure the air was clean, couldn't protect him from invisible threat. I'd lost it—control, the fraying ability to keep myself in line.

The next day I took the X-Acto knife out of my desk drawer and put it downstairs, far from my reach. [My past illness of] anorexia was one thing; being comforted by the appearance of my blood was another.

I called my analyst, the one I'd seen for ten years, the one I stopped seeing the last time I was pregnant, when, buoyed by the life I carried, I grew impatient with examining old wounds and graduated myself prematurely. "I need to talk to you," I told her.

The Therapeutic Relationship

Because my analyst had recently had a knee replacement, she was working out of her apartment, a place I'd never visited. My years of weekly treatment had been conservative, formal, and necessarily one-sided. My analyst was as strict as she was sympathetic, and in all that time we had never embraced, had rarely touched. I was afraid to see her home because I preferred her unknown and unknowable. My relationship with my own mother had been damaging enough that, forty-one years old, I remained vulnerable to older women, prone to fervent attachment and unreasonable hurt. In my analyst's carefully polished therapeutic mirror I'd found the reflection of wishes and fears long hidden. I'd depended on its clarity and did not want it tarnished; nor did I want to be given any snag on which my neediness might catch.

As it turned out, I hardly saw the apartment. The sight of her face—the proximity of help—was so potent a catalyst for tears that I saw nothing.

"You know you need to be on medication," she said, after I'd told her about the past two months, admitting everything: the obsessive worrying; the unwarranted conviction that I had made my son sick; the insomnia; the fear of annihilation that plagued me; the seductive calm offered by the sight of my blood; the complex of rules pertaining to food, a quagmire from which I'd nearly escaped again and again, more times than I could count.

Getting Help

"You're not forgetting what happened before," my analyst prompted, alluding to my stubborn refusal, in 1998, to resort to antidepressants, pride that insisted I deny depression until it dismantled me.

"No," I said. "I remember."

We scheduled an appointment for the following week, and in the meantime I saw my internist to get prescriptions for Paxil (an SSRI that relieves anxiety), Wellbutrin (a mood elevator), and enough Xanax to tide me over during the weeks before the first two took effect. It was a familiar arsenal. Together my doctor and I acknowledged that I was thin; there was ten pounds less of me than there had been six months before, when I'd had my yearly physical. But, expecting the drugs to do their job, we didn't belabor the observation.

In the month before the antidepressants kicked in, I had a few panic attacks, a blight I recognized from my earlier breakdown. At least I no longer mistook them for cardiac arrest or cerebral hemorrhages or organ failure. These did have the new feature of beginning with a burning sensation all over my body, as if every inch of my skin had been scoured with Ben-Gay. Then my heart beat fast, faster, too fast—it would have to stop or break. Floors tilted, ceilings pressed down, menacing swaths of red swung open and shut like phantom theater curtains, showing me either too much or too little. Language and music refused to cohere into anything I could understand but came at me broken into scrambled, mocking bits. And the attacks lasted an hour or more, long enough to drench my clothes and hair with sweat, fold me into a fetal position, and leave me witless.

Searching for Answers

Each time I saw my analyst, we reviewed my son's improving health and then, inevitably, returned to the subject of breast-feeding, and the depression that had arrived in May, when I'd stopped nursing and lost a bond that, I'd begun to admit, protected and soothed me as much as it had my children. Without nursing—without the hope of ever nursing again—I had a sense of being stalked by a black, destructive force. My son's illness suggested to me that this invisible predator was drawing closer. It was only a matter of time before it got me. But what was the black force? As had previous fears, this one dragged our conversations back to what I called my "failure to connect" with my mother.

The Relief of Medication

John Falk

John Falk is a journalist and writer who has suffered from chronic, severe depression his entire life. In the following excerpt from his book Hello to All That: A Memoir of War, Zoloft, and Peace, *Falk describes the period in his life just before he was put on Zoloft, the drug that finally lifted his depression. Having just enrolled in graduate school, Falk writes, he became sunk in a deep, unrelenting depressive episode that included thoughts of suicide. Only thoughts of his parents and especially his mother kept him from acting on those thoughts. Falk recalls taking Zoloft for the first time and experiencing intense relief from what he describes as ten years of painful depression.*

I kept my dreams of self-annihilation to myself because I didn't want to worry anyone. I'd already done enough of that; I had already put everybody through too much. But some things don't have to be said. It was clear I wasn't functioning at all, and my very presence in the heart of my family was poisonous. My mother was so consumed with worry, she barely slept. My father, trying to hold the whole show together, was at his wit's end. Then circumstances intervened. My mother became very ill and had to undergo serious back surgery and my father's business was struggling. They decided they had no choice but to sell the house. Needless to say, my attic sanctuary was going to go with it. I was about to lose my last mooring.

Despite my condition, my father had talked me into applying to graduate school for the fall semester of 1992. "You got to go. You got to make it work," he told me. "For yourself and for your mother. You've got to make a life for yourself." His desperation was as plain as the fact that he could no longer watch what my illness was doing to my mother.

I knew he was right but I was terrified, in pain, literally, at the thought of losing the one place in the world where I could feel . . . comfortable, really, yet at least protected. But then again, my father was right. This couldn't go on. I had to get a life. Plus, the damage I was causing to those closest to me was ratcheting up my rediscovered self-hatred. What finally made me agree was my father's conviction that if I went to school and really applied myself, great things were bound to happen. As he spoke, I could almost see what he envisioned. I wanted to believe in his dream, too, but I had wanted to believe in lots of things.

"You sure?" I asked him. "You sure about this?"

"Absolutely, kid," he told me. "Trust me, I know what I'm talking about."

Always a sucker for a new beginning, I bought into my old man's vision as best I could.

In the fall of 1992 I found myself down in Charlottesville, enrolled in the graduate program in foreign affairs at the University of Virginia. Upon arrival, my only priority was to find the right place to live. I didn't care about the location or amenities. The only thing I gave a damn about was that my new home had bookcases, enough space to hold the two hundred and fifty books that filled my car. These books were my security blanket, and I eventually found a room that had once been the library of a big, old Victorian house right off fraternity row.

Once I had moved in, I spent a week decorating: arranging the books by subject matter; taping a pheasant-patterned fabric to the box spring of my bed to make a dust ruffle; centering my desk in front of the bay window; scouring the local Salvation Army thrift shop for just the right furniture; tacking up Monet and van Gogh posters along with a school banner;

and topping it all off with a Persian rug knockoff and an array of Boston ferns and philodendrons. Up to that point the verdict was still out, this whole enterprise was still all possibility, but it had to start and my energy was actually kind of surprising.

Dressed in khakis and a button-down oxford, I attended my first round of classes, a week late, and quietly collected all the handouts I had missed. Back in my room, I organized them on my desk, took a hot shower, got dressed, poured a cup of coffee, rolled up my sleeves, sat at my desk, and got down to work. The first of the Xeroxed documents was a survey of the ethnic makeup of southeastern Europe. Bulgars. Roma. Magyars. Romanians. Serbs. Greeks. Turks. Croats. Bosnians. Something called a Slovene. It took only a page for me to start panicking: *What the f - - - am I doing? What's the point to all this? Where is this going to get me? What am I doing here?*

It was odd but I was back where I started, pretending to be normal to anyone who cared to inquire but privately living in a nightmare. My parents called every day when I was down in Virginia, and every day I told them everything was going great. But four months after I arrived in my new home in Charlottesville, that is, in January 1993, I was holed up in that old library turned bedroom. By then it was the start of the second semester, but the truth was I had never finished the first. Two months into my return to academia, I was barely hanging on. Some days I was so defeated and down I couldn't even scrape together a decent reason to move—not for class, bathing, or food. Other days I would make it out the door, but not actually to class.

When I did make it, about half the time, I never said anything and these were graduate classes, chock-full of people who were supposed to be passionate about the subject matter. Not only didn't I give a shit, I felt like a seven-foot, four-hundred-pound, eight-legged alien in a human's mask doing my best to remain undetected. I lived in abject fear that one of these professors would call on me and find me out, which, of course, eventually one did.

"Mr. Falk, we haven't heard from you yet. Maybe you'd like to give this a try?" the professor asked one day, referring to something he had written on the blackboard.

By that point in my life I had felt like an Other for over ten years. My sense of alienation had grown so intense that it had consumed everything in my brain. When that professor asked, "Maybe you'd like to give this a try?" all I can say is I felt like the whole world, all six billion people, was looking at me. I didn't move a muscle.

"Mr. Falk, maybe you'd like to give this a try?" he asked again, as if I hadn't heard him.

What he was asking was actually not that complicated, but I just couldn't speak, even to say no.

"Come on, give it a try," he said.

I starting sweating. I felt it beading on the back of my neck. My heart was racing. I barely managed to shake my head.

"You sure?" he asked.

I lowered my head.

"OK," he said. "Maybe someone else would like to give it a try?"

At the end of class, the professor asked me to see him in his office. Walking over there, I thought I was totally screwed. I didn't belong in that school. I didn't even know what I was doing there, but if I got booted, I couldn't even imagine where else I could go. At least here, I was still alive on paper, technically doing something. So, when I finally got in there and he told me to take a seat, I was expecting the worst.

"Do *you* want to be here?" he asked straight out.

"Look, I don't know," I told him. "I wish I I could tell you absolutely yes, but I can't."

"Then why did you come here?" he asked.

"I mean, don't get me wrong, I'm interested in this stuff," I said. "Look, I don't know if this means anything, but a while back someone diagnosed me with depression and maybe that, maybe that has something to do. . . ."

He held up his hand, shook his head, and said, "Don't say any more. That's all I needed to know. Depression is a serious illness, and I'll work with you no matter what it takes. You're in this school now, John, and we'll all work with you."

I was amazed at his empathy. As soon as he heard me say "depression," he felt he had his answer. He hadn't told me I was crazy or trying to shirk something. This professor, this perfect stranger who owed me nothing, somehow intuitively knew that I wasn't so much a graduate student as someone who was just holding on for dear life, and having him say in so many words, "Don't worry, I'll help you," meant everything. It was a little bit of light at a very dark time.

So that January, the start of the second semester, I was a quasi-graduate student: going to class, but not taking exams. Most days I just sat in my room, staring out the window or watching video tapes of the history of Poland between the world wars. These tapes infuriated me because these Poles were fighting back and forth, shedding blood and arguing over all these fine points of government, national identity, economy, religion, and for what? I felt like yelling at the television every time I watched one, "You're fools. It doesn't matter. In a few years, the Nazis are going to show up. Then Stalin. It's all meaningless."

Before Virginia, I was in one of my deep episodes where I couldn't even get out of bed. I wasn't eating. I wasn't sleeping. All I had the energy to do was imagine my own death. About three days into it, with no end in sight, I reached out to my mother. She was in her room, folding laundry. As soon as I walked in, she tried to give me a smile but it was obviously forced. She was as desperate as I was.

"Ma, what do you believe in?" I asked her.

"What do you mean?"

"I mean, why do you do what you do?" I asked. "What do you believe in?"

She took a seat on the bed and took a deep breath. "I believe . . ." she thought for a second. "I believe in being good, that we all matter."

"What does that mean? All matter? How could that be?"

"What don't you understand?" she asked me.

"All of it."

"John, life is short. It can be hard, trust me. But we all matter to other people. What we do matters to other people. At the end of the day, that's what matters. Being a good person."

"But that doesn't make sense," I said. "Why does it matter? Who cares?"

"John, it does matter," she said. "It's the little things we do for each other that make life. Maybe it doesn't make sense, but it matters. Let me ask you: What do you believe in?"

"Nothing."

"What do you mean?" she asked.

"I mean, I don't believe in anything."

"Nothing?" she asked, shaking her head, almost as if she didn't believe me.

This anger, this pure venom, just welled up in me and I screamed, *"Ma, I don't believe in anything!"* And as I yelled that, I whipped the phone against the wall, shattering it. My mother put her head in her hands and wept. I put my hands to my head because I knew I had become a monster. I leaned down and hugged her, and she seemed so small and frail.

"I'm sorry, Ma. I'm so sorry," I said. "I would never hurt you."

"John, just tell me, even if you have to lie, just tell me you'll be all right."

"Ma, I'm gonna be fine," I lied. "Trust me."

In truth, by then I had actually come to believe in something but I didn't want it to be true. Life was just brutal. It wasn't fair. No one was promised happiness. Virtue wasn't necessarily rewarded, vice punished. It was all just a crap shoot. Some lost, some won. And for whatever reason, I had lost.

Sitting in that room down in Virginia that January, in that carefully reconstructed replica of my attic, that was how I pretty much had come to see it. I was defective. There was something wrong that prevented me from simply living. But deep down I didn't think it was depression per se, some faulty chemical interaction in my brain. It was *my* fault. I was the only person living my life, making the choices I made. I was the one who had built this prison for myself, a prison no one else could see. Most others couldn't understand, which made it all the worse. Who the f - - - was I to feel this way, anyway? I had nothing to complain about, yet that's all I did. Everything was negative. Empty. Without value. I was on this planet sucking up resources but producing nothing. I was excess baggage. If I had it my way, I would have been dead already.

One day, I remembered [a] box I found in the crawl space off my attic bedroom when I was a kid. I thought of the kid in the cowboy outfit who turned out to be my uncle Robert. I remembered my mother's sad words when she described him: "On the edge of other people's lives." He never had anyone; his own mother had abandoned him to his fate. He had died alone "on some stupid beach in Eureka," as Mom had put it.

"On the edge of other people's lives." That was me and this was now. In Virginia, I didn't know anyone well anymore. I had made no friends. I didn't make plans with anyone. I had a cousin who lived only a block away—a star athlete at UVA whom I had been close to growing up. But I never saw him. I had friends from home who had younger brothers at school down here. I never saw them. The point was, I didn't want to see anyone. When I did get caught, I would always do just enough to ward off any questions and then disappear back into my cocoon. Back there, safe and alone, I would find myself envying Robert. "*Dying alone on some stupid beach in Eureka.*" That sounded nice to me. I wanted to be that lone photo stashed away in someone's attic. I wanted to disappear. But if I took my life, the pain I would inflict on the very people pulling for me, believing in me, would outweigh the intense misery I experienced every day. And that's the only reason I chose to keep my heart beating at this time. I had truly been beaten because I finally gave in for good: I was never going to be part of the world.

Before I left for Virginia, I had asked my mother, among other things, not to worry about me. A ridiculous request, and, of course, she ignored it. She stayed in touch with Dr. Atchley, mostly to keep him up to date on how I was doing and keep abreast of any new developments. As luck would have it, around that time a new antidepressant hit the market. In clinical trials, it had proved particularly effective with unipolar depressives like me. It was called Zoloft, and my mother called to tell me that Dr. Atchley, who had recently semiretired and moved up to Massachusetts, thought I should go to the student health clinic to get a prescription. As my parents and Dr. Atchley were the only people I still trusted completely, I did.

I went on Zoloft in January 1993 and for a few weeks nothing changed. When Dr. Atchley had put me on Prozac a year earlier, I had asked him, "How will I know it's working?" He had said, "You'll just know."

It was a few days before Valentine's Day, and I have no clear recollection of how I spent the night before. Probably like always, I was just lying in bed, staring at the tube, utterly alone, running through the same loop of unanswerable questions. I probably knocked off at my usual time, two or three in the morning.

When I awoke, it was after ten. With the pillow over my head, and still a little groggy, I remembered I had a class at eleven. Plus, I still had those damn Polish tapes in my possession, a good two weeks overdue. If I hustled, I could return the tapes and still make it to class. I rolled out of bed, and as I hadn't bathed in a few days, I took a quick shower. I put on some pants, an Irish sweater, a jacket, grabbed the tapes, a notebook, and ran out the door. I walked down the driveway, turned onto fraternity row, and headed to campus. It was one of those rare winter days, sunny and brisk. It was a quarter-mile walk to the video store and I don't remember thinking that much in particular. But I'll never forget what happened as I was crossing over a little graffiti-covered bridge. I smelled wood smoke. It was as simple as that. I smelled wood smoke, and suddenly I had this feeling of being this little kid again, running home in the winter, through the snow, it's dark, my nose is ice cold, my hands in balls, but I know at home everyone is there, hanging out. It will be warm when I get home.

And that was it.

"You'll just know," Dr. Atchley had told me.

And he was right. I just knew at that moment that it was over.

I stopped and turned around and around and looked at everything. Nothing had changed. Everyone was just walking along as they had been. The only difference was, I wasn't on the outside watching. I was just simply part of it all, part of life. Nothing more, nothing less. I doubled over, put my hands on my knees, and let out a breath I had been holding inside myself for ten long years.

A Story of Teenage Depression

David L. Marcus

David L. Marcus is an education writer and foreign correspondent who has written for the Boston Globe *and* Vanity Fair *among other publications. In 2001 Marcus spent time with students at the Academy at Swift River, a boarding school in Massachusetts for adolescents with emotional problems. He describes the experiences of four in his book* What It Takes to Pull Me Through. *This excerpt focuses on the experiences of Tyrone, a teenager who suffers from depression. Marcus tells the story of Tyrone's upbringing, including his father's drug addiction and subsequent arrest, which contributed to Tyrone's depression. The excerpt then shifts to Swift River, in a wilderness portion of the program, in which Tyrone struggles with his feelings of loyalty to his friends and deep-seated fears of abandonment.*

EVERY NIGHT, the kids in base camp elected a leader for the next day. Time after time, they voted for Tyrone. Just as he'd promised, he finished everything he started. He didn't whine or throw tantrums; he didn't alienate anyone by spreading gossip. Between breakfast and lunch, most kids went through the gamut of emotions—giddiness, dejection, outrage; cursing their parents and then missing their parents—but Tyrone remained reassuringly stoical. Once in a while he flashed a contagious smile after finishing PT or chores. He didn't admit it, but he found base camp relaxing. He felt a sense of accomplishment when he won a race, hauled the most logs, or checked off a box in his growth book after finishing a chapter of *Jonathan Livingston Seagull*. After three weeks, the counselors made him a hawk—the highest level at base camp. Just a few more days and he'd move to campus.

During group therapy, though, Tyrone faded into the tree trunks. Andy, the boy from Long Island, pointed out that whenever someone asked about Tyrone's father, Tyrone refused to say anything negative.

"That's because I don't have anything negative to say," Tyrone said.

"But what kind of things does your dad do with you?"

"He plays basketball with me."

"How often does he play?"

"Well, my mom usually won't let him come over."

"When you were little? How often did you play basketball with him?"

"Sometimes. A few times. He worked nights so he slept during the day."

Andy cocked his head and gave a don't-bullshit-a-bullshitter scowl. He asked why Tyrone's father barely even visited. Tyrone said that his mother had gotten an order from a judge. Some kind of protection order, because she didn't like his father.

The counselors said Tyrone needed to be a real part of the group. That meant talking honestly instead of ignoring others or feigning ignorance. They put him on spice bans and told him he had to shake hands every morning with each student and counselor while looking everyone in the eyes.

Ashley, the button-nosed girl from Manhattan, was a city kid through and through, and she made Tyrone laugh (one morning she let loose a blood-curdling scream when she awoke to find a chipmunk cuddled up in her sleeping bag). It was a short subway ride from Tyrone's block in Queens to Ashley's place on Park Avenue, but they might as well have been on different continents. Tyrone lived in a cramped house and went to a public school so large that he didn't know the names of most of his classmates; Ashley lived in a building with white-gloved elevator operators and went to an elite private academy where some kids got dropped off by limousine.

Tyrone and his friends saved up money to go to video arcades; Ashley went to thirteen-year-olds' parties that featured singers who had been on MTV. Tyrone's most memorable vacation had been at Disney World; Ashley spoke with authority about the Louvre.

Still, Tyrone and Ashley connected when they talked about what food they missed the most. They both loved McDonald's. Not Burger King or Taco Bell. Just McDonald's.

"I always get number four," Ashley said.

"Me, too. Double Quarter Pounder and fries."

"*Ho!* [I hear you]" Ashley said. "With Coke."

"Sprite."

There in the woods, a two-hour hike from the nearest fast-food restaurant, they found a bond. Tyrone would have a friend when he made it to main campus. That was reassuring for someone who had felt alone for as long as he could remember.

In Tyrone's world, not much was reassuring. His mother, Natalie, had grown up in a Harlem railroad flat, sharing a bedroom with her two brothers. Money was so tight that they scrounged in garbage cans to find cardboard to insulate their shoes. Natalie's father worked in a plant that made amphetamines for pharmaceutical companies. The amphetamine dust seemed to affect him; after work he had extreme ups and downs. Natalie's stepmother was a bitter woman who ordered Natalie to shut up when she hummed while doing the dishes. Natalie wanted to go to college but went to work instead at age eighteen. She married Lerone, a college dropout who had studied computer programming. They had a daughter and then a son, Tyrone. Their firstborn was so accustomed to getting all the attention that she completed Tyrone's sentences. As a toddler, Tyrone simply stopped speaking for several months—a practice he resumed in adolescence.

Natalie cooked, cleaned, and worked full time as a technician at the phone company. She had never relied on anyone, and she wasn't about to rely on her husband. It was she who found out about a Korean couple who had been burglarized and couldn't wait to leave Queens. Natalie paid $30,000 for their home, a tiny, two-story frame house. It faced the intersection of two busy avenues and looked squarely at the Projects. The view out back was even worse—a bus depot. But she owned it free and clear. Natalie took off the iron grills that covered the windows because she hated to feel she was imprisoned in her own home. If some junkies wanted to steal the family's meager possessions, then let them (someone did just that, breaking a back door and hauling away a stereo and jewelry).

Tyrone's childhood memories were a blur. His mother's account of those days contrasted so sharply with his father's that Tyrone no longer knew what was true. Most of what he'd heard came from his mother. She claimed that Lerone used heroin. When Tyrone was six, the family went to a Fourth of July party thrown by Natalie's relatives. Lerone huddled with a group of men in an alley the whole time. Strange things started to happen after that. Lerone removed himself even more from family life; he started working the overnight shift and spent the days in bed. His bank account, which had grown to $18,000, dwindled to zero. Natalie would come home with cash in her pocketbook and half of it would soon disappear. While doing the laundry, she emptied Lerone's pants pockets and found vials of powder that looked like Comet. Several times, Lerone locked himself in the bathroom and then emerged, leaving blood in the sink. Thinking back on the party, Natalie had a queasy feeling. A relative told her that one of her brothers-in-law had introduced Lerone to cocaine that day.

Lerone constantly announced his good intentions. He wanted to take Tyrone to the movies, to the zoo, to a ball-game. But he usually arrived late or didn't show up, and the plans rarely turned into reality. He had a friend who was an accountant, and they sat in the kitchen coming up with moneymaking schemes while Natalie bustled around them cooking and cleaning. She learned to tune them out—just as she tuned out a lot of other things that were going on around her. One night, she came into the bedroom and saw Lerone hunched over, snorting something. She walked downstairs without saying anything. Lerone followed her to the kitchen and said he was just using occasionally. Natalie turned on him. "You do what you want, but when you stop doing your job, which is providing for the children, you'll find skid marks on your butt from sliding down the street. That's how fast you're gonna be moving when I throw you out."

According to Natalie's version of events, Lerone was laid off and life got worse. After more money vanished, Natalie began tucking her cash in her bra and sleeping with it. Lerone withdrew money from the ATM, forgetting to tell Natalie, who tracked every cent in the household. Lerone signed up for one credit card after another and racked up $26,000 in debt. Then a letter arrived from the IRS: The Harristons were being audited. They needed to present proof of the medical expenses they'd deducted for treating Tyrone's sickle-cell anemia.

"Sickle-cell *anemia*?" Natalie sputtered. She had let Lerone and his friend do the taxes and she'd signed the 1040 without looking at the details. "You're so sick that you used your own son for tax fraud!"

The IRS slapped them with a $6,000 fine and another $8,000 in penalties. Because Lerone had no money, the government put a lien on Natalie's bank account. Signing a tax return without reading it was not an excuse and she lost the money. In the middle of the financial mess, a woman called frequently, looking for Lerone. The woman sounded strung out on something or other. "I have two children but the BCW took them," she volunteered, referring to the Bureau of Child Welfare. Natalie didn't know what the woman wanted from Lerone, nor did she care. She likened herself to a subway-commuting, cooking, dishwashing zombie, dazed from one shock after another, such as the fire that consumed their house. Actually, there wasn't a fire—but Lerone and his accountant crony had invented a roof-melting, wall-buckling inferno for the IRS. They were audited again.

One day when Tyrone was nine, he looked up from television to see two cops handcuffing his father and dragging him out of the house. Natalie explained that she had filed for divorce and had gotten a judge's order of protection to ensure that Lerone kept his hands off her. "Don't you see what your father's been doing?" Natalie asked Tyrone. Natalie's brother-in-law had died of a seizure after drinking, and several of her relatives and neighbors had overdosed on drugs. She said Tyrone's dad had an illness called addiction. She took Tyrone to a Narcotics Anonymous meeting, but he was too young to understand.

Barricading himself in his little room, Tyrone refused to talk or eat. He could wait. After all, his father had sworn he'd return and straighten things out. Every month or two, he showed up to take Tyrone and his sister out for ice cream. He emphatically denied using drugs and said that Natalie was a bad mother. Tyrone, unsure of what to believe, became increasingly withdrawn. He was cranky in the mornings when it was time to walk to elementary school. It was an old brick building with hissing boilers and windows that didn't close all the way. After school, Tyrone would let himself in at home and watch television or play Nintendo. He wasn't allowed to have friends over without adult supervision, and he followed the rules. Parents want compliant children, but Tyrone was almost too compliant; he was listless all the time, and he showed no interest in anything other than video games. Natalie fretted about her son's long, lonely afternoons, but she had to pay the bills, and that meant keeping her job at the phone company.

At night, she and her daughter would fix dinner and Tyrone would eat alone in front of the TV in his six-by-eight-foot bedroom.

Tyrone advanced from grade to grade mostly because he sat quietly in the back of the room without stirring up trouble. But when he reached eighth grade, New York City announced it would abolish the tradition of social promotion. To move to the next grade, students would have to pass their classes and standardized tests. Tyrone squeaked into ninth grade at a five-story high school that took up a city block. The school had 3,900 students; two-thirds of them were so poor that they got free or subsidized lunches. Tyrone hated passing through metal detectors every time he entered, he hated the catcalls that echoed through the halls, and he hated the fights that broke out over the smallest provocation. Before teachers could learn his name, Tyrone decided high school wasn't for him. He'd stay awake till four or five in the morning, take a nap, then wolf down breakfast and walk around the block. As soon as Natalie left for work, he'd sneak back home and go to sleep until five in the afternoon. Every day, a computer would call the house and announce that Tyrone had been absent from school. Tyrone let the answering machine take the call, then pressed the erase button.

Although Natalie suspected her son was cutting some classes, she didn't realize he was skipping entire weeks of school. No one showed an interest in him. Natalie went to see a truant officer who made it clear that he didn't care whether Tyrone showed up or not, though he explained that he wanted to keep Tyrone's name on an enrollment list so the school wouldn't lose several thousand dollars in per-pupil funding from the district. Natalie went to the Board of Education offices to argue that Tyrone needed to be moved to a special program with small classes because he had a learning disability or depression. The specialists rebuffed her. Tyrone wasn't disruptive or dangerous; he wasn't classified as "at-risk." They implied that he was just a shiftless teenager with a lazy mother.

Natalie eventually remarried, a man who had been drafted to Vietnam and had risen from private to corporal in the army, then finished his tour of duty on the brink of becoming a sergeant. After the war, he'd married and raised three daughters. Although his first marriage didn't last, he prided himself on being a father who was caring as well as strict. He tried to be a good influence on Tyrone, too. He took the boy bowling and shooting pool, things Tyrone had never done before. He took Tyrone to his first Yankees game. Tyrone went along but didn't exchange more than a few words with his stepfather. He was waiting for his dad to come home.

Natalie kept promising Tyrone that she'd make more time for him, but life got busier. Tyrone's sister, who wasn't married, had a baby. Natalie, still trying to raise Tyrone, found herself a grandmother at age forty-seven.

Tyrone had a small, loyal group of friends. There was Paco, his Puerto Rican friend from childhood, and Lance, who was getting ready to go into the army. And Black Manny—not to be confused with Fat Manny, who was Mexican, or Little Manny, an eight-year-old Italian boy who sometimes followed them around and imitated them. Little Manny cracked them up, bellowing "Yo, niggah!" as if he were the big man on the block. On the night before Tyrone had to leave for [the school in] Massachusetts, the guys came over to the house. They hung out drinking Pepsi in the living room, which was so small that their knees bumped when they sat on the sofa and the two easy chairs that faced it. Tyrone had a few CDs, all featuring parody artist Weird Al Yankovic.

After a while, they left Tyrone's house and walked past the Projects and over the footbridge that connected Queens to Roosevelt Island. Roosevelt Island was a development in the East River between Queens and Manhattan that tried to have the flavor of an old-fashioned city, with apartments over stores and parks out back. Tyrone and his friends liked the south end, whose old, abandoned buildings were perfect for exploring. They walked through a crumbling structure emblazoned with gang graffiti. Tyrone didn't talk about the fact that he was being sent to a boarding school—a "go-away school," he called it. The other guys wondered how he would stand being stuck in the sticks with a lot of rich white kids. Paco said Swift River sounded like a military academy. Paco had credibility: He had gone to school every day in ninth and tenth grades, while Tyrone stayed in his bedroom.

"You never did homework," Tyrone countered.

"I didn't do nothing. But I passed, right?" Paco said. "Now look where they're making you go. See, you shoulda went to school."

On a torrid afternoon in late August, with the drought well into its third month, the kids from Group 23 sat in a circle on the parched grass for a therapy session with the base camp counselors. Andy coughed and cleared his throat and said he had to come clear about something. Everyone waited. Had he tried to sneak a Heineken out to base camp? Was there a secret he had hidden from his parents, something horrible he'd done at home?

"I have to be honest," he said in his deep voice. "I took two apples at breakfast."

It was pure Andy. He'd confess to something almost for the sake of confessing. No one was very impressed by his newfound conscience. Stealing a piece of fruit or a hunk of cheese at base camp now and then was like smoking a joint at home; almost everyone did it. Still, Andy's confession led Ashley to say that she, too, needed to clear up something. Maybe she was inspired by Andy; they'd been watching each other and flirting in not-so-subtle ways. Something about Ashley's quivering voice caused everyone to stare. It was apparent that she was going to own up to something more serious than, say, ripping off an apple.

"I was going to run away tonight," she said.

"*Was?*" one of the counselors asked.

"I'm not. Not anymore."

The counselor asked if she was sure. Yes, she said, she'd decided to stick out base camp. Running wouldn't make things better. Anyway, Ashley conceded, her plan wasn't much of a plan; it involved walking on a path down the hill and listening for the sounds of cars. When she found a road, she'd have hitched a ride to New York.

The counselor asked her if she'd shared her plan with anyone. She hesitated.

"Who was it?"

Her eyes got teary.

"Who?"

She looked down. "Tyrone."

All eyes turned to Tyrone, who sat stone-faced.

Ashley explained that she had approached him while they were pumping water. She'd made sure no one else could hear. "Can you keep a secret?" she had whispered. "I'm going to run tonight."

"That's crazy," Tyrone had said. "You can get lost. What happens if you trip? Who's gonna find you?" Ashley had thought about it and promised she wouldn't run.

The counselors' attention switched to Tyrone. They asked if that was how it had happened. Yes, he said. "Do you realize what you did?" scolded a counselor. "You jeopardized the safety of the group. What's the most important thing here?"

Tyrone was silent.

"Safety," the counselor said. "You're about to finish up and go to campus. Hawks are supposed to set the example here. Why didn't you tell us that Ashley was planning to run away?"

"Because she promised me she wouldn't."

How did Tyrone know Ashley wouldn't run? Why didn't he alert a counselor? Hadn't he heard that other kids had taken off in the middle of the night and had to be rescued?

Tyrone's face looked contorted. He held up his hands and started crying. It was the first time anyone at base camp had seen him cry. He said that he didn't want to tell on Ashley because she was a friend. He shook and wheezed as the tears fell. "I've only had three friends in my life," he sobbed. "I didn't want to lose a friend."

The counselors told Tyrone that he would have to spend an extra three days at base camp, working on writing assignments. Before moving to main campus, he needed to understand more about what had happened in his childhood that made him so fearful of being abandoned. Tyrone reacted by sitting stiffly and looking straight ahead, his arms crossed.

Before going to sleep, he wrote a poem in pencil. He titled it "Lonely Once Again."

Where you going? Can I come?

I want to follow. I cant. Why not?

Your voice is getting softer. You must speak up, you have to tell me why.

No not again. I am all alone.

I hate this feeling. Why me? Always me.

The people who left me are the only people who cared.

Tyrone didn't show the poem to anyone. During the first days in base camp, he'd resolved not to tell other kids about his life and his feelings. Now he'd learned a valuable lesson: He didn't even want to hear about their lives or their feelings. Somehow he'd keep his head down and get through this crazy school. Anyway, he was just here for the academics.

My Experience with Deep Brain Stimulation

David Beresford

In the following narrative, author David Beresford recounts the unexpected result of a brain stimulator implanted in his head to alleviate the symptoms of Parkinson's disease. He awoke one morning after having the stimulator adjusted to find himself very happy and prone to bouts of uncontrollable laughter. Exploring the situation, Beresford's doctors informed him that the device was currently being used to help depression that would not respond to other treatments. Beresford writes that in his opinion, this device could bring great relief to the suffering of those caught in deep depression. David Beresford, a correspondent for the London newspaper the Guardian, *is based in Johannesburg, South Africa.*

About three weeks ago I walked into the rooms of my brain doctor in Cape Town [South Africa] carrying a bunch of flowers. "These are for you," I said. "You've made my speech worse and I suspect you've screwed up my balance. But what you've given me has a price greater than rubies."

I am blessed with the attendance of a number of brain doctors around the world for the Parkinson's disease I suffer. The most important are in Grenoble, France, where a couple of years ago a neurological team buried some electrodes deep inside my brain and connected them up to a pacemaker under the skin of my chest.

The idea was that by sending a small electrical current into my brain they could stop the shakes, which are the main symptom of Parkinson's. It worked like a dream. Not only were the shakes gone, but the stiffness—another symptom of the disease—as well. But, being human, it did not take long before I felt that it was not enough (we are an ungrateful lot, but then it can be said that therein lies the genius of our species). My speech was becoming worse and it was time it was fixed, I felt.

One of the problems with my near-magical brain operation is that most of the experts are in Europe and I am in South Africa. There is only one person who performs the operation in this part of the world, and he is the surgeon in Cape Town. Ideally, I should be treated post-operatively by a neurologist and not a neurosurgeon. But the two of us make do. If I have a problem I see him at first and then head for Europe if he cannot help.

A few days before presenting him with flowers, I had been in to see him, complaining about the deterioration in my speech. He fiddled around with a magnetic switching device used to do these things and off I went, after promising to report back and tell him if there was any improvement.

That evening, I happened to be speaking on the telephone to my youngest son in Holland when something he said started me laughing. To my embarrassment, my giggles would not stop (after all, one likes to maintain a degree of decorum with one's youngest). Eventually, I had to say a hurried goodbye and cut the call short.

It was not until the following day that I began to realise that something fairly fundamental in me had changed. And not only in me, it seems, but for mankind.

Experiencing Depression

Last year, I had visited my neuro-team in Grenoble. At the end of the session, I raised the issue of depression. Was I depressed? And if so, was it a result of Parkinson's disease, or of the operation and the pacemaker? The neurologist proceeded to cross-examine me, asking—among other things—whether I had thoughts of suicide. "Heavens, yes," I replied, "often. But I have no intention of committing it."

I should perhaps explain here that I saw suicide (or so I told myself) as a philosophical issue. My mother-in-law, with cancer and in her 90s, recently opted for euthanasia and carried it out with extraordinary courage and single-minded determination. My father had been trapped, by a series of strokes, in that awful place from which one can no longer communicate with the world. Suffering a degenerative disease myself, I would be almost remiss if I never thought about it. But depressed? Me?

"Yes," said the French neurosurgeon. It was not serious, but could become so and he prescribed an antidepressant. Back in South Africa, I dutifully took the drugs, but when they had failed to have any significant effect after several months I took myself off them.

Which is pretty well where things were when I arrived in the rooms of my Cape Town brain doctor, demanding that he do something about my speech.

The day after my fit of laughter on the telephone to my son, it began to dawn on me that my life had changed, radically. An overcast day was no longer cause for despondency, but a glorious change in the weather. I used to wake at 9 a.m. in the morning, sometimes at 11 o'clock, but now I was waking at 5 a.m. and—after nervously taking mental stock— couldn't (or wouldn't) go back to sleep.

I hurtled down the lower slopes of Table Mountain on my bicycle into the city centre, frightening the children and local dogs by my attempts to yodel as I went. In the lovely old building that is the South African national library, with its banks of computers, I dived into the Internet. "Deep brain stimulation" and "depression," I asked Google.

And there was the answer.

DBS Can Help Depression

"They're using deep brain stimulation to treat depression," I told my Cape Town brain doctor, with wonderment. "I don't know anything about that," he replied candidly.

"The Canadians seem to be leading the way," I said. "You must have done it by accident."

I sent a hurried email to Grenoble, telling them what had happened. Back came the reply in the form of a lengthy message, with attachments from learned journals. It is an astonishing story, contained in those journals, which can perhaps best be told by starting with a paper published by the journal *Neuron*, earlier this year.

In the paper, Dr. Helen Mayberg and colleagues from Toronto University reported the discovery that a small area in the frontal cortex [of the brain] is implicated in depression. Application of electrical stimulation to the area had "striking and sustained remission" in four out of six patients suffering treatment-resistant depression.

The implications are extraordinary. As they observe, "treatment-resistant depression is a severely disabling disorder with no proven treatment options once multiple medications, psychotherapy and electroconvulsive therapy have failed." Not only does it offer a means of treatment for tens of thousands, but—in the words of one senior neurologist—"this paper really is the beginning of the return of psychosurgery." Which is enough to have me, and no doubt many others, offering up a short prayer to the international neurocommunity: "Please, guys, just don't screw it up this time." Because last time the screwup was spectacular, thanks to Freeman and Moniz.

Walter Freeman and Egas Moniz are two names that are likely to be forever associated with a pioneering form of psychosurgery. The story of lobotomy is well known. But, briefly, Moniz won the Nobel Prize in 1949 for the medical breakthrough on which lobotomy was based. Unfortunately, the prize had the effect of giving an imprimatur [approval] to Freeman's performance of the operation.

Freeman, in effect, ran amok, using an ice pick to separate the pre-frontal lobes of his patients. It was said that his surgical technique was so upsetting to observers that seasoned physicians would collapse in his operating theatre with nausea. Thousands suffered his attention, the most famous being the beautiful actress and political activist Frances Farmer, who was lobotomised on the grounds that she was too much of a rebel against authority.

DBS—Induced Laughter

Another paper I received from France threw some light on my mirth during that telephone conversation with my son. It was published three years ago by the journal *Movement Disorders* and written by my Grenoble neuro-team, Paul Krack et al. The authors included the two leaders of the unit at the University of Grenoble, the surgeon Alim-Louis Benabid and the neurologist Pierre Pollack, who have become internationally renowned through their development of what I call my "pacemaker operation"—technically known as deep brain stimulation (DBS) of the subthalamic nucleus (STN), which is fast becoming the standard treatment for advanced Parkinson's.

The paper's title is self-explanatory: "Mirthful Laughter Induced by Subthalamic Nucleus Stimulation." If emphasis were allowed, it would be on the word "mirthful."

As the paper points out, pathological laughter is known to be associated with neurological disease, including epilepsy. The difference was that "the laughter attacks reported in this paper were associated with humour, appreciation, and mirth".

The paper describes the cases of two patients on whom they had experimented by raising the stimulation levels to a point where laughter and associated dyskinesias (uncontrolled movements) were induced. One of the patients seems to have

Depression

been particularly witty. The laughter was highly infectious and
several neurologists who were present in the room also fell
into a hilaric state.

"For example, when looking at the nose of Professor Benabid, the patient thought of the nose of Cyrano de Bergerac (as
he told us later) and started another burst of laughing, pointing at Professor Benabid's face.

"When Dr. Krack could not restrain himself any more and
fell into a burst of laughter, the patient shouted, 'Il craque' (he
cracks up, which puns on the doctor's name) and this pun led
to a generalised burst of laughter of all the people present, including the patient."

In both cases, extreme stimulation resulted in improve-
ments in mood, motivation, libido—and a general enjoyment
of the pleasures of life.

Will my improvement follow their course and my newfound happiness be sustained? Every morning, when I wake
up, I repeat that nervous stocktake to find out. My big worry
is, of course, the fear of mood swings. The thought of being
as unhappy as I am now happy is a frightening one. Laugh as
one may, the jury of researchers is still out. Although most
pointers are positive, there have been cases where the operation seems to cause depression, rather than alleviate it.

"What goes up must come down," well-intentioned friends
often advise me. The Twin Towers admittedly came down, but
what the hell, the Golden Gate Bridge, the Empire State Building, Big Ben and the [South African] Voortrekker monument
are still standing, aren't they?

CHAPTER 3

Treatments
for Depression

An Overview of Alternative Therapies

Aviva Patz

Aviva Patz is a freelance writer specializing in health and mental health issues. She has written for Health *and* Psychology Today, *as well as for the Lifetime television channel. In the following article, Patz provides an overview of alternative and natural treatments for mild and moderate depression. Many people don't consider alternative therapies, she writes, yet many have been shown to be as effective as traditional methods such as talk therapy and antidepressants. Patz discusses the pros and cons of herbs such as St. John's wort, light therapy, exercise, and acupuncture and provides quotations from people who have found these methods helpful in alleviating their depression.*

During the summer, her symptoms always improved slightly, says Cynthia Eicher, a 43-year-old working mom from Minnesota. That pattern made her think there might be a natural approach to her years-long battle with moderate depression. So she traded in one of the antidepressants she was taking for a light box, and she now feels like a new woman. "I can finally appreciate the two kids I love, a husband I adore, and a really good job," Eicher says. Some 21 million Americans—twice as many women as men—suffer from depression. According to a Harvard Medical School survey, two-thirds of the respondents who saw a conventional provider for depression also used alternative therapies like relaxation techniques, herbs, vitamins, and yoga to treat the condition—and more and more doctors are taking notice.

"We're seeing a lot more interest from conventional medical centers regarding natural remedies for depression," reports psychiatrist Jonathan E. Alpert, M.D., associate director of the depression clinical and research program at Massachusetts General Hospital. "To not study them would be a great disservice, partly because there are limitations to existing treatments."

Indeed, nearly half the population taking antidepressants have only a partial response or none at all—and as many as 30 percent to 50 percent suffer adverse reactions, says Alpert, including fatigue, weight gain, sexual dysfunction, nausea, headaches, and dizziness. Preliminary studies suggest that certain natural remedies may increase the effectiveness of some antidepressant drugs or replace them altogether.

Finding one or more alternative remedies that work for you may take some trial and error, and should be done in consultation with a mental-health practitioner. Whichever path you follow, get eight hours of sleep a night and spend time with people who will support your healing objectives.

Benefits of Exercise

Exercise enables both body and mind to break free of rigid, negative patterns. It stimulates nerve growth and produces energizing, feel-good brain chemicals, such as endorphins, adrenaline, serotonin, and dopamine. In addition, working out promotes feelings of accomplishment and control and helps break the vicious cycle of sluggishness and depression.

Thirty to 40 minutes of aerobic exercise three to five times a week can cut the symptoms of minor to moderate depression nearly in half, according to a 2005 study in the *American Journal of Preventive Medicine*. "The results were comparable to antidepressant treatment and psychotherapy," says lead author Madhukar Trivedi, M.D., professor of psychiatry and director of the mood disorders program at University of Texas Southwestern. An earlier study at Duke University Medical Center found that exercise was as effective as the antidepressant Zoloft in reducing or eliminating mild to moderate depression.

Aim for 30 to 40 minutes three to five times a week of intense aerobic exercise, such as fast walking, running, or cycling. It takes two to four weeks to feel a measurable effect and around 12 weeks to see a significant improvement, notes Trivedi.

The suicide of her 33-year-old son plunged Kathy McKinney into a profound depression. Antidepressants helped briefly, but the symptoms came back—and didn't lift again even after the doctor increased her dosage. A friend urged her to join a study on exercise and depression at the University of Texas. McKinney, a 57-year-old resident of Emory, was assigned to ride a stationary bike and work out on a treadmill 20 to 30 minutes three times a week for 12 weeks. "After a few weeks I noticed that I felt a bit better," she says. "Little by little, I came out of that depressing fog.". . .

Regulation Through Supplements

One of the better-known supplements for depression is S-adenosylmethionine, but even after about 40 clinical studies, researchers still don't know exactly how SAMe works. According to Alpert, the prevailing theory is that it may increase the activity of neurotransmitters thought to be involved in mood regulation, including serotonin, norepinephrine, and dopamine. SAMe also helps build nerve membranes, which make nerve cells more efficient at sending signals, and synthesizes glutathione, an antioxidant that may increase mood-boosting chemicals available to the brain.

A 2002 review of SAMe studies, published by the United States Department of Health & Human Services, found the supplement equal to at least low doses of some antidepressants, and with fewer side effects (mild gastrointestinal upset, headaches, and insomnia). A 2004 report in the *Journal of Clinical Psychopharmacology* showed that adding SAMe to standard medication improved symptoms for half the participants and produced complete relief in 43 percent of them.

"SAMe is a promising substance that may offer other avenues of treatment for people who either don't respond to conventional antidepressants or prefer to start with a natural substance," says Alpert, who led the study.

Studies have used dosage ranging from 800 to 1,200 milligrams twice daily. You should feel a difference within two to three weeks, notes Alpert.

Diagnosed with clinical depression at age 21, Gina Jozaitis, now 34, tried nearly ever antidepressant available. All of them left her feeling groggy and spaced out; one made her sleep for 40 hours straight. Less than a week after the Cicero, Ill., resident started taking SAMe, she felt better than she had in years. "The darkness lifted," she says. Four years later, she's still taking SAMe daily and would never again consider a prescription antidepressant.

Conventional Ways: Therapy and Drugs

Talk therapy and antidepressants are still the first line of defense for many doctors who treat depressed patients. Psychotherapy can change negative thought and behavior patterns that trap you in a cycle of depression. A 2005 study in the *Archives of General Psychiatry* found that 16 weeks of cognitive therapy may be as effective as antidepressant medication in the initial treatment of even moderate to severe depression; it also helps prevent relapses.

Additionally, talk therapy improves the success rate of antidepressants, according to a 2002 study in *Biological Psychiatry*. By themselves, these drugs can cut depression symptoms in half for roughly 60 percent of patients, says Ronald Pies, M.D., clinical professor of psychiatry at Tufts University Medical School and author of the *Handbook of Essential Psychopharmacology*. "When appropriately prescribed and monitored, the medications can be lifesaving," he says. "But they should be integrated into a plan that addresses social, psychological, and even spiritual issues."

Antidepressants increase the amount or enhance the function of neurotransmitters in the brain. Progress can usually be seen in three to five weeks, and in some cases longer.

Help from Herbs

While a number of botanicals can affect mood, the leader of the pack is St. John's wort (Hypericum perforation). Investigators believe it boosts the amount and efficacy of serotonin in the brain's hypothalamus and hippocampus, and may help the brain better absorb other mood-enhancing hormones.

Much of the research on St. John's wort—pro and con—has been flawed. A well-regarded double-blind study published last year in the *Journal of Clinical Psychopharmacology* concluded that the herb is in fact "significantly more effective" and has fewer side effects than fluoxetine (Prozac).

With your doctor's approval, take 300 mg of St. John's wort three times a day. You should see a gradual improvement in six weeks.

Frustrated with the side effects of pharmaceuticals (especially the sexual dysfunction they caused) and wanting to feel more in control, Nancy Schimelpfening, 41, of Oceanside, Calif., tried St. John's wort nine years ago. While it took longer to kick in than the drugs had, the herb proved just as effective for Schimelpfening and caused her zero side effects. "After three months I was sold, and I haven't been significantly depressed since," she says, though she continues to take the herbal remedy off and on when she's feeling blue.

Unconventional Means: Four More Options

Homeopathy Although its exact mechanics are unknown, homeopathy is characterized by Bernardo Merizalde, M.D., a psychiatrist in Lafayette Hill, Pa., as a kind of negative feedback loop. "We give the body a very small amount of a substance that can cause the same symptoms as the problem when given in large doses," he says. "This signals the body to correct it."

There are hundreds of homeopathic remedies, but a practitioner will narrow these down based on your condition. For example, sepia works best on people who withdraw, isolate, and refuse to be consoled. Pulsatilla, on the other hand, is preferred for patients who tend to be weepy and want to be consoled.

Since treatment is so individualized, you'll need to see a licensed practitioner.

Acupuncture This ancient science is thought to alleviate depression by stimulating the synthesis and release of norepinephrine and serotonin. In a study at the University of Arizona, two-thirds of the participants found significant relief from depressive symptoms after a short course of acupuncture. Two studies carried out in China have shown that electro-acupuncture, where the needles are electrically stimulated, is as effective as some antidepressants. To treat mild depression, most patients get acupuncture twice a week for up to eight weeks.

Massage Therapy Apart from how good it feels, a massage alters brain patterns and chemical production. The hands-on treatment also enhances relaxation, which improves sleep—a depression fighter in itself. In a recent study, depressed pregnant women received 20-minute massages twice a week. After 16 weeks, the subjects, who reported feeling less anxious and depressed, had higher levels of serotonin and dopamine and lower levels of the stress hormone cortisol. A moderate-pressure 20-minute body massage twice a week from a professional or your significant other can provide respite from mild depression.

Spirituality Faith is a powerful antidepressant, say two Duke University scientists who recently found that depressed older patients with greater religiousness recovered 70 percent faster. Two-thirds of the data reviewed found that religious people have less depression than their nonreligious peers, and that if they do get depressed, they recover more quickly. "Religion gives people hope and helps them overcome negative life experiences," says lead researcher Harold G. Koenig, M.D., professor of psychiatry and behavioral science at Duke University Medical Center and author of *New Light on Depression*.

You can add a spiritual component to your life in a variety of ways: attending formal prayer services; participating in a yoga retreat, drumming circle, or kabbala seminar; or volunteering through your local church or religious community.

Omega-3 Acids and B Vitamins

The foods you eat—or don't eat—have a great effect on how you feel mentally. Low levels of different minerals, including zinc, magnesium, and iron, have been found to play a role in regulating mood, but the most promising research focuses on omega-3 fatty acids and B vitamins.

A recent animal study from a Harvard-affiliated hospital found that consuming omega-3 fatty acids and uridine—two substances occurring naturally in cold-water fish, walnuts, and other foods—could have the same effect as taking drugs. "The findings suggest that omega 3 can be useful in treating some depression," says lead author William Carlezon, Ph.D., associate professor of psychiatry at McLean Hospital in Belmont, Mass. "Omega-3s and uridine enter into the brain's cell membranes and make them more fluid and flexible so they can produce more energy and function better."

Also, clinical studies have shown that people with depression often have low levels of many B vitamins, including B^9 (folic acid)—and the greater the deficiency, the greater the depression. The B vitamins help regulate neurotransmitters like serotonin, norepinephrine, and dopamine.

For maximum impact, Andrew Stoll, M.D., an associate professor of psychiatry at Harvard Medical School, recommends taking 1 to 2 grams daily of eicosapentaenoic acid (EPA), an omega-3 fatty acid found in fish oil. To get this much EPA, you may need to double or even triple the dose of fish oil recommended on the label. But according to Stoll, studies suggest that EPA is the active omega-3 component in fish oil, and it's important to dose according to the active ingredient.

Meanwhile, keep your diet rich in omega-3S (salmon, grass-fed beef, enriched eggs, flax) and in B vitamins (fortified breads, whole grains, lean meats, fish, dried beans, peas, soybeans, eggs, milk). Steer clear of omega-6 fatty acids (fried foods, corn and soybean oils), which incite inflammation and counteract the omega-3 benefit.

Brianne Glidden, a clinically depressed 51-year-old from Houston, had sampled every class of antidepressant ever made. "Either it would just stop working or I'd have nasty side effects, mostly bad headaches," she says. Then, on the advice of a therapist, she started adding omega-3 supplements to her drug regimen, which allowed her to take better advantage of her counseling sessions and helped eliminate the side effects. Today, Glidden combines daily omega-3s with very small doses of Zoloft, and the combination is working. "I've never felt so clear-headed and content," she says.

Receiving Light Therapy

Daily exposure to artificial light of 10,000 lux (a measure of illuminance) of white light is a standard treatment for Americans who suffer from seasonal affective disorder, a winter-related depression. It reduces symptoms in 60 percent to 80 percent of those who try it, says George C. Brainard, Ph.D., a professor of neurology at Jefferson Medical College in Philadelphia. New data indicate that light therapy also helps with nonseasonal depression, with or without medication.

A 2005 review in the *American Journal of Psychiatry* showed that light therapy is comparable to antidepressants for treating many mood and depressive disorders. (The researchers weeded through 173 published studies and included only the 20 they judged were done properly.)

The mechanism of the treatment's success is unclear. Brainard suggests that light received through photoreceptors in the eye may help enhance the response to serotonin. Another explanation is that the light alerts the body to stop producing melatonin, a hormone associated with sleep. For most people, melatonin shuts off automatically, but dark winter mornings can muddle people's internal clocks and may set off a series of physiological responses that lead to depression.

Sit in front of a large light panel for 30 to 60 minutes first thing in the morning, advises Brainard. You can be reading or eating breakfast as long as you are near the light-emitting surface and look up at it every minute for a few seconds. Or get some natural light therapy by taking a walk outside every morning, which a Swiss study in the *Journal of Affective Disorders* has shown to lift symptoms. If you don't see an improvement in one to two weeks, light therapy may not work for you, says Brainard.

After a week of treatment, Minnesotan Cynthia Eicher noticed a difference; by the third week she felt better than she ever had. Eicher still takes a half-dose of antidepressants a day, but "for someone suffering for years and years with depression, this is truly incredible," she says.

Yoga and Meditation

Long promoted as a technique to reduce anxiety and stress, meditation (and meditative movement like yoga) can help you control your emotional state and improve resilience. "Meditation teaches you to pay attention and respond more effectively to your body's feedback," explains psychologist David Tate, Ph.D., director of the Center for Stress Reduction in St. George, Utah. Mindfulness techniques help you perceive and release negative or judgmental thoughts and turn your attention to more positive perceptions. "The process of recognizing, acknowledging, and then redirecting helps you stop the cycle of ruminating, which can lead to depression," Tate says.

Mindfulness meditation, which teaches the practice of living in the moment, produces lasting positive changes in both the brain and the immune system, according to a 2003 University of Wisconsin study published in *Psychosomatic Medicine*. Also, a UCLA study in progress indicates that mild to moderately depressed patients who attend hour-long yoga classes three times a week for eight weeks show significant decreases in symptoms of depression and anxiety. "Certain kinds of bodily changes, like opening the chest and backbends, may increase circulation to the brain and affect mood," says study leader David Shapiro, Ph.D.

Play an instructional tape on mindfulness meditation for 15 to 20 minutes a day either during yoga practice or by itself. You may feel results after one session, but it takes six to eight weeks to experience major improvement, Tate notes.

After a very difficult breakup, Shelley Scholzen, 49, of Hurricane, Utah, couldn't sleep, lost weight, and felt utterly hopeless. At the urging of her twin sister, who had used meditation to combat her own depression, Scholzen signed up for Tate's nine-week class on mindfulness meditation and yoga. Before the first session ended, she started feeling better. "It was amazing," she says. "It helped me tune in to myself and feel complete. I experienced so much joy I finally felt some peace." Although she's no longer depressed, Scholzen still practices mindfulness techniques every day, during her evening walks and in her regular yoga workout.

Varieties of Psychotherapy

Harvard Women's Health Watch

In the following article from the Harvard Women's Health Watch, *a newsletter from Harvard University Medical School, the authors provide an overview of types of psychotherapy, how to decide if therapy would help, and how to choose a therapist. "Talk" therapy is effective on its own, or combined with antidepressants, the authors explain. It is generally divided into two areas: psychodynamic therapy, which focuses on the past and unconscious memories and thoughts, and cognitive-behavioral therapy, which helps patients learn techniques to combat their particular stress or problem. Whichever approach is chosen, the authors write, it is important to choose an experienced, properly trained therapist with whom you have a strong rapport.*

Every year, one in five adults in the United States experiences a mental disorder or an emotional problem serious enough to warrant treatment. Although psychotherapy is a cornerstone of psychological treatment, the initial suggestion—whether it comes from your physician, spouse, or best friend—can raise many questions. Are my loved ones tired of discussing my problems? Does my doctor think I'm crazy? Can talking really help? Would medicine work just as well? Will my insurance help pay? How do I find the right person to talk to?

Psychotherapy—often referred to as talk therapy—addresses troubling symptoms and emotions using psychological techniques rather than, or along with, medication or other physical approaches. There are many theories and styles of psychotherapy, but the two most popular forms are psychodynamic therapy and cognitive behavioral therapy.

Which works best? There's no simple answer. Just as many forms of aerobic exercise can help you achieve cardiovascular fitness, many types of therapy can help you understand yourself better, change behavior that is wrong for you, and help relieve bothersome symptoms. You may do better with one type than with another, or find that a blended approach, drawn from different schools of psychotherapy, suits you best. Your regular participation in the process is more important than the type of therapy you choose. Most important is the match, or rapport, between you and your therapist.

Although most therapists emphasize one type of intervention, a good therapist can incorporate elements of others as well. Whatever approach the therapist adopts, she or he should develop a trusting alliance with you, suggest fresh ways for you to perceive your problems, and help alleviate your symptoms and your sense of isolation.

Psychodynamic Therapy

Psychodynamic therapists believe that past experiences and feelings of which you're not consciously aware can influence your present emotional well-being and ability to function. Through regular discussions with a therapist, you can gain insight into your motivations and conflicts and learn more productive ways to cope with them.

"Psychodynamic therapy can be very helpful if you feel like your life is repeating old patterns or you aren't clear what direction you want to take," says Harvard Medical School psychiatrist Margaret S. Ross, M.D.

The process of psychoanalysis developed by Sigmund Freud may be the most familiar form of psychodynamic therapy, but it's not the most common. Psychoanalysis is designed to uncover the unconscious roots of your symptoms and help you apply this understanding to your current life. Classic psychoanalysis is time-consuming (it requires meeting several times a week, possibly for many years) and not widely used today. However, it's still influential in the thinking behind much psychodynamic therapy, which can be short- or long-term, and may focus broadly or more narrowly on a particular issue or symptom.

Another common focus of psychodynamic therapy is an individual's interaction with other people. Psychodynamic therapy can help you identify what you seek in a relationship (your needs), the healthy and unhealthy ways of meeting those needs, and ways to improve your ability to communicate. Such therapy can help people cope with the loss of a relationship, conflicts within relationships, or the demands of shifting roles (such as retirement or caring for a parent). One system of therapy with this emphasis, called interpersonal therapy, combines elements of psychodynamic therapy, cognitive behavioral therapy, and other techniques. Therapy is limited to three or four months and focuses on psychological difficulties sparked by recent conflicts or transitions. While not widely available, it is coming into more common use.

The Cognitive Behavioral Approach

Cognitive behavioral therapy (CBT) is less focused on the underpinnings of feelings and instead emphasizes how to change the thoughts and behaviors that are causing problems. CBT can be used to alter difficult behaviors, such as smoking, procrastination, or phobias, and can also help address conditions such as depression and anxiety.

Cognitive behavioral therapists believe that you can change your feelings by changing your thoughts and actions. For example, you may have patterns of distorted thinking—excessive self-criticism or guilt, always anticipating the worst, attributing untoward motives to others—that make you vulnerable to feeling bad. CBT teaches you to recognize these patterns as they emerge and alter them. The "behavior" part refers to learning more productive responses to distressing circumstances or feelings—such as relaxing and breathing deeply instead of hyperventilating when in an anxiety-provoking situation.

Other Forms of Therapy

Most talk therapy involves one-on-one meetings with a psychotherapist, but other configurations can be helpful, too, depending on your needs.

Group therapy Several people meet in regular sessions with a therapist. Interacting with others and hearing their problems can support your efforts to change and reduce your sense of isolation. Group therapy can be particularly helpful for people with difficulties in social interaction because it provides a place to practice and get feedback from others. A group may be organized around a single topic, such as anxiety, bereavement, or a medical condition—or it may be concerned with more general issues, on the understanding that most people cope with similar problems.

Before joining a group, you will be interviewed by the therapist and may be asked to commit to a certain number of sessions. Group therapy may be combined with individual sessions.

Family therapy This involves the family unit. It's usually brief and focused on problem solving. It can help families correct miscommunication, change dysfunctional patterns of blame, or adjust to altered circumstances, such as a chronic illness or adult children moving back home. It may be especially helpful when an individual's psychological problem affects other members of the family.

Couples therapy Also called marital therapy and marriage counseling, couples therapy focuses on your relationship with your partner. The process may be much like individual psychotherapy, or the couples therapist may act as a mediator, finding acceptable compromises when there is conflict. The therapist helps you and your partner examine your patterns of interaction and determine what changes are needed for each person to be satisfied.

Support groups Support groups are usually organized around a specific issue, such as bereavement, a particular illness, divorce, or recovery from addiction. A professional usually does not lead them, and, strictly speaking, they are not a form of psychotherapy. But they can be extremely helpful for individuals or families confronting certain circumstances or striving to sustain healthy behavior changes. Like group therapy, support groups may be time-limited or ongoing. Insurance doesn't cover all support groups.

Match Therapy with Problem

While medications are essential for the adequate treatment of certain mental disorders, such as schizophrenia, bipolar disorder, and severe depression, research shows that improvement is often greater when psychotherapy is added. By helping you understand and cope with the disorder, talk therapy can also help you stay in treatment and avoid relapse.

Anxiety disorders can be treated with psychotherapy, medication, or both. CBT is the most common treatment for phobias, that is, irrational fears of certain objects or situations. If you have generalized anxiety or obsessive-compulsive disorder, CBT can help you learn to respond differently in situations that cause anxiety. A combination of psychotherapeutic approaches is required to help people with posttraumatic stress disorder (PTSD) come to terms with their trauma, losses, and painful memories.

Either talk therapy or medication can be used to treat mild to moderate depression, but combining them may be particularly effective. For example, researchers at the University of Pittsburgh School of Medicine found that when depressed people ages 60 and over received psychotherapy along with an antidepressant, they were symptom-free longer. Their quality of life and social interactions improved more than those of patients receiving either treatment alone.

Recent research comparing before-and-after brain scans of people being treated for depression suggests that medication and psychotherapy counter depression in different ways. Among people receiving psychotherapy (as CBT), PET scans showed increased blood flow in the limbic, or "emotional," system, and decreased activity in certain "thinking" areas of the brain. Subjects who took antidepressants showed different changes in the same brain regions. This may help explain why individual responses to treatment vary so much.

For seasonal affective disorder, a type of depression that recurs in the fall and winter, the standard approach is regular exposure to bright light. But new research indicates that CBT may work just as well, by helping patients revise their negative thoughts about the lack of light and learn ways to cope with winter darkness.

After diagnosing depression, a primary care doctor is more likely to prescribe an antidepressant, and a psychiatrist is more likely to recommend psychotherapy and an antidepressant. (A psychiatrist is also more likely to prescribe the antidepressant at the correct dose for you.) Your preferences should be considered. If your primary care physician prescribes an antidepressant, you can request a referral for psychotherapy, or wait to see how you respond to the medication, which may help you participate more effectively in talk therapy.

A psychiatrist may both provide psychotherapy and prescribe medication, but most psychotherapists cannot prescribe drugs. If you're seeing a non-M.D, psychotherapist, she or he may recommend that you ask your physician about a prescription for an antidepressant. In that case, it's important for the therapist and prescribing physician to collaborate in providing the best care for you.

Omega-3s and Depression

Patrick Perry

In the following article journalist Patrick Perry interviews An-drew Stoll, a researcher who has shown that doses of omega-3 fatty acids can alleviate the symptoms of both depression and bi-polar disorder. Omega-3s are found in certain kinds of fish, Stoll explains, and can prevent certain kinds of diseases caused by in-flammation, such as heart disease, arthritis, and stroke. Omega-3s produced anti-inflammatory hormones, which Stoll believes, is the reason they can also help depression and bipolar disorder. Patrick Perry writes on health issues for the Saturday Evening Post. *Andrew Stoll is a professor of psychiatry at Har-vard University.*

[In 2002] Dr. Andrew Stoll, director of the Psychopharma-cology Research Laboratory at Harvard Medical School-McLean Hospital, conducted a landmark study on the role of omega-3 fatty acids in bipolar disorder and came up with some surprising results. The researcher discovered that when patients with bipolar disorder consumed omega-3 from fish oil, they experienced a marked reduction in episodes of mania and depression. Extensive research continues to demonstrate that omega-3 fatty acids form the foundation of a solid, healthy diet, while also reducing the risk of heart disease, stroke, hypertension, and arthritis, among other conditions.

Depletion of the essential omega-3 fatty acids in the typi-cal American diet is linked to chronic disease and the huge in-crease in the rates of depression. Researchers now speculate that the increase in depression correlates well with the pro-gressive depletion of omega-3s in our diet throughout the 20th century. The shift from rural community life to fast-

Patrick Perry, "Battling the Blues," *Saturday Evening Post*, vol. 277, May–June 2005. © 2005 Saturday Evening Post Society. Reproduced by permission.

paced urban sprawl also ushered in an era of fast foods, low fiber, and foods high in saturated fats, trans-fatty acids, and excessive intake of omega-6 fatty acids.

Omega-6 fatty acids are converted by the body into a number of strongly inflammatory hormones, collectively known as eicosanoids. Prostaglandins are the most well-known class of eicosanoids. If omega-6-derived eicosanoids are produced in excess over time, the risk of developing heart disease, other inflammatory medical conditions, and, apparently, depression and bipolar disorder skyrockets.

The omega-3 fatty acid eicosapentaenoic acid (EPA) is converted into eicosanoids as well, competing directly with omega-6 fatty acids for access to the enzymes that convert these fatty acids into eicosanoids. Whichever acid wins the competition for these eicosanoid-producing enzymes depends solely on the ratio of omega-6 versus omega-3 consumption in the diet. This is crucial, because the omega-3-derived eicosanoids are largely anti-inflammatory hormones and have the role of keeping the omega-6-derived eicosanoids in check. Now, omega-6 fatty acids aren't bad, unless there is an excess over time.

Therefore, essential fats such as the omega-3s EPA and docosahexanaenoic acid (DHA) are necessary for optimal health.

Historically, scientists believe that our ancestors consumed close to a one-to-one dietary ratio of omega-3 found primarily in certain fish, to omega-6, commonly found in vegetable and seed oils. Today, researchers estimate that the ratio of omega-6 to omega-3 fatty acid consumption is somewhere between 20:1 and 50:1 in the United States, with an abundance of omega-6 over omega-3 fatty acids, which pushes us in a pro-inflammatory direction, more susceptible to heart disease, arthritis, and to illnesses related to inflammation, and perhaps depression and bipolar disorder.

To update readers about Dr. Stoll's ongoing research into the role of omega-3 fatty acids in depression, the [*Saturday Evening*] *Post* spoke with the Harvard researcher and author.

An Interview with Andrew Stoll

Post: Do omega-3 fatty acids continue to demonstrate mood-stabilizing benefits?

Dr. Stoll: No one has replicated the findings of our original study as yet. The real story now is that there are now numerous positive studies on the benefits of omega-3 in unipolar depression, schizophrenia, borderline personality disorder, ADHD, and Huntington's disease. It seems that many disorders respond to omega-3s. Three of the four studies in depression used EPA, or EPA plus DHA, and they worked. The fourth study used pure DHA—important for developing babies, pregnant women, and nursing mothers—and it failed. People hold onto stores of DHA for a long time, so you don't need to replenish levels as often as with EPA, which is turned over constantly, by conversion into eicosanoid hormones.

Post: Does EPA have anti-inflammatory properties?

Dr. Stoll: Exactly. The anti-inflammatory action of omega-3s has been definitively shown to help prevent heart attacks, in part by reducing atherosclerosis (hardening of the arteries). Omega-3s also appear to help cut down on the need for medications to treat rheumatoid arthritis, ulcerative colitis, Crohn's disease, and a number of other medical conditions. Omega-3s may also work in osteoarthritis. Research on omega-3s is exploding—and not just in psychiatry.

Post: Are you continuing your research into the relationship between fats and mental health, particularly omega-3 fish oils in bipolar disorder?

Dr. Stoll: Yes. We published the results of our first bipolar study, and the results were very promising. We went out on a limb to do this study with no funding and with colleagues sometimes ridiculing us. But the study was logical and rational, and patients, as well as informed and open-minded physicians, liked the approach. We tried it randomly and it worked. The same pathways are activated during bipolar disorder and depression, so EPA may perform the anti-inflammatory action.

Post: Do your patients, who were part of the original study, continue to take omega-3 and experience relief from their symptoms?

Dr. Stoll: I still see some of these people. All continue to take omega-3 supplements. In my practice, I am in favor of it, so I advise people to take it—if not for the psychiatric benefits, then for the general health benefits.

Post: Is there a downside to supplementing with omega-3?

Dr. Stoll: There isn't. Some people may experience GI distress if they take a large amount of a low-quality supplement. But the highest good-quality fish oil is not rancid and has little or no taste and has no side effects. Another issue that people worry about is bleeding, because EPA inhibits platelet aggregation. But we scoured the scientific literature, and there has never been a documented case of bleeding due to omega-3 fatty acids.

We recently reviewed about 18,000 people who participated in clinical trials with omega-3s, largely in cardiology studies, and we couldn't find one instance of bleeding in any of the trials. There was no bleeding, even if used in IVs prescribed before and during cardiac surgery. I think this perception is a myth because omega-3s don't inhibit the platelets as strongly as aspirin—perhaps 60 to 70 percent as much as aspirin—and unlike aspirin, the effect is reversible.

Post: When a patient is on blood thinners, such as coumadin, should they exercise caution when supplementing with omega-3?

Dr. Stoll: In that situation, I usually recommend a lower dose, not exceeding one or two grams of EPA per day. At this dosage, there should be no effect on the action of coumadin.

The unanswered question is, together are they providing too much anticoagulation? Nonetheless, there may be some minute risk of a negative interaction with anticoagulants, such as warfarin (coumadin), high-dose aspirin, or ibuprofen-like medications, based on animal data and anecdotal reports in humans.

However, large-scale controlled clinical trials with patients receiving omega-3 fatty acid supplements with either aspirin or warfarin observed no cases of bleeding even after one year of the combined treatments. It would be a shame if cardiac patients or their physicians avoided the use of omega-3 supplements out of fear. I am thoroughly convinced that the dramatic and lifesaving cardiac actions of omega-3s far outweigh the very small or nonexistent risk of bleeding.

Dosage for Depression

Post: What dosage do you recommend for patients with bipolar and/or depression?

Dr. Stoll: Our omega-3-fatty-acids-in-bipolar study was the first controlled study in psychiatry. We really had no way of knowing what the minimum effective dosage was, so we decided to use a moderately high dosage that had been successfully used in omega-3 studies of rheumatoid arthritis and other medical disorders. This dosage was about 10 grams per day (6.5 grams of EPA and 3.5 grams of DHA daily). Most of the newer omega-3 studies in major depression used a very low dosage of pure EPA added to partially effective or noneffective antidepressants. For example, in one small study, Dr. Malcolm Peet and colleagues from England compared one gram a day of EPA to two grams a day of EPA, and up to four grams of EPA per day. One gram of EPA did the best by far. The most recent depression study, done by a group from Taiwan, was another unipolar study where they added omega-3 to an antidepressant regimen that was not working. They used the same exact formulation that we did—nearly 10 grams of EPA plus DHA in about a 3:2 ratio—with good results.

So, the question of optimal dosage remains unanswered. Practically, I start patients on one gram of EPA per day, and go up on the dosage gradually until an effect is seen on a person's mood. I usually do not have to exceed six grams of EPA per day. The amount of omega-3 in a supplement may be calculated from the side of the bottle.

It is important to know that the amount of active ingredients in supplements is listed on the label by serving size, not necessarily by how much of an ingredient or compound is in one capsule. Companies can make the serving size one, two, three, or a hundred capsules—as big or small as they want.

To determine omega-3 content, simply take the amount of EPA or EPA plus DHA per serving, as listed on the label, and divide it by the serving size to determine how much omega-3 is in each capsule. That's not understood well by many people. It is important that people read labels carefully. They get fooled.

The FDA requires that supplement manufacturers list the ingredients or nutrients by serving size. But the company can put in any serving size they want, so it may look like there is a lot of EPA, for example, in a product, but the serving size may be 10 capsules. Consumers should be sure to divide whatever value is in the column for the amount of EPA by the number of capsules in a serving, and read labels carefully.

Post: What dose of omega-3 do you recommend and find most effective?

Dr. Stoll: I will distinguish the doses. I usually start everyone on one gram of EPA per day. I prefer to have a little bit of DHA in the formula. They should be at least in a 3:2 or 2:1 EPA to DHA ratio. If one gram doesn't help after one to two weeks, I will raise the dosage to two grams a day of EPA. I definitely use lower doses than I used to, based on the depression data. Occasionally, someone will call or e-mail me with an anecdote that they didn't respond until they were taking 10 grams a day—the original dose in our study. Hopefully, we will resolve that issue in the next few years.

Post: When consumers are looking at supplements, what is the ideal ratio of EPA to DHA that they should look for?

Dr. Stoll: This remains an unresolved issue, but I like a 7:1 ratio of EPA to DHA. That high ratio delivers plenty of EPA—the presumed active ingredient—and also provides an adequate amount of DHA. More DHA is required during pregnancy or while nursing to replenish stores. Most adults and children seem to have adequate or nearly adequate stores of DHA in their brains. Believe it or not, these DHA stores in the membranes of brain cells date back to a person's fetal life and is provided by their mothers. DHA turns over very slowly, so you don't need much to get by. In contrast, EPA is turned over very rapidly, as it is used for eicosanoid synthesis. For this reason, we think people are also much more depleted in EPA than DHA.

Understanding Transcranial Magnetic Stimulation

Dennis O'Brien

Dennis O'Brien is a science writer for the Baltimore Sun. *In the following article, he reports on transmagnetic stimulation (TMS), a new treatment that relieves severe depression. TMS, O'Brien explains, involves applying a magnetic field to the brain. The field can be directed to the part of the brain responsible for depressive feelings, quieting it. However, O'Brien writes, the treatment is only being used in trials in the United States, and has not been approved by the FDA. It carries a risk of seizures; only patients with depression that is unresponsive to other treatments can be considered for a trial.*

Editor's note: As of February 2007, TMS was still under review by the FDA.

As a mother of five who sang in a church choir and ran two businesses near Philadelphia, Garrett Aguilar considered herself happy.

But she also knew that depression ran in her family. When she began to show symptoms [in 2002] her doctors tried a variety of standard treatments—six months on Prozac, a week on Wellbutrin and a year on Zoloft. Nothing could restore her spirits.

"I just found myself getting deeper and deeper. It got so bad I couldn't get out of bed," said Aguilar, 55, of Berwyn, Pa.

Then a friend mentioned an experimental treatment that sounded almost like science fiction. Called TMS—for transcranial magnetic stimulation—it attacks depression by applying a magnetic field to the brain.

She enrolled in a TMS clinical trial at the University of Pennsylvania School of Medicine—a site for one of two major TMS studies in recent years. The study was funded by a firm seeking federal approval for the first TMS device specifically designed to treat depression.

If approved, it could offer hope to the 4 million people who suffer from depression but fail to respond to standard therapies or can't tolerate the side effects, said Dr. Mark Demitrack, a psychiatrist and medical director of Neuronetics Inc. of Malvern, Pa.

"There's no question that what's out there now just doesn't work for everyone," Demitrack said.

Researchers have been exploring TMS for two decades, using a technique that can sound bizarre to the uninitiated. The test subject sits in a chair while a scientist places a magnet on his head, then sends magnetic pulses through his skull to "light up" various areas of the brain.

As strange as TMS seems, depression can be so debilitating that patients who fail to respond to other treatments are willing to try almost anything.

A Profound Change

That's how bad things were for Aguilar by Christmas 2004, when she found she didn't even have the energy to decorate her house for the holidays—a ritual she always enjoyed. "I was at a point where I felt like I had nowhere else to turn," she said.

After participating in the six-week randomized trial, Aguilar agreed to a follow-up round of TMS treatments. "It kind of tickles your scalp," she remembered.

After a few weeks, she began to improve. These days, she takes a low dose of Lexapro, an antidepressant, and hasn't had a TMS session since March 2005. She credits the magnetic therapy with curbing her depression.

"TMS absolutely changed my life," she said. "It might not work for everybody, but it certainly worked for me."

Researchers are still refining their techniques. They know that by placing the device on different areas of the head, they can make fingers twitch or freeze speech in mid-sentence. There is a small risk of seizures.

But in preliminary studies, TMS has stilled imaginary voices in the heads of the mentally ill and shown promise for treating headaches, post-traumatic stress and obsessive-compulsive disorders.

"It sounds like sci-fi, doesn't it? But I think this is big news," said Dr. Sarah H. Lisanby, a TMS researcher who is director of brain stimulation at Columbia University College of Physicians and Surgeons.

Doctors interested in treating depression aim the magnets at the prefrontal cortex. Other researchers target areas controlling speech, memory or the nerve centers that bring on migraine headaches.

Researchers at Ohio State University Medical Center released a study last week showing a hand-held TMS device placed against the back of the head reduced the pain of migraine headaches. There is no risk of seizures because the device sends out only single—and not repeated—magnetic pulses, said Robert Fischell, the Howard County inventor who developed it. A clinical trial is planned for this year and Fischell hopes to win Food & Drug Administration approval and begin selling the device by mid-2007.

Focus on the Brain

Last year, scientists at Yale University reported the benefits of applying TMS to brain areas controlling speech perception in 50 schizophrenic patients who were having auditory hallucinations. When researchers focused the magnetic field on what is known as Wernicke's area, the imaginary voices subsided. Their report was published in *Biological Psychiatry*.

"You can shut off specific brain functions, things like speech or motor control," said Dr. Eric Wassermann, chief of brain stimulation at the National Institute of Neurological Disorders and Stroke, a branch of the National Institutes of Health.

In 1998, after a small number of TMS test subjects reported seizures from repeated pulses, Wassermann published safety guidelines dealing with the frequency and duration of the magnetic pulses used in TMS research.

There remains a small risk of seizure, a risk also found with several depression medications. But Wassermann considers the technique safe enough to practice on himself. He experimented a few years ago by having a fellow researcher target the speech centers of his brain as he was speaking. A few zaps of TMS stopped him from talking in mid-sentence.

"It was an indescribable feeling," he said.

There are several standard treatment options for depression. Over the years, drugs such as Prozac and Wellbutrin have helped millions cope. Electroconvulsive therapy, also known as ECT or shock therapy, has also been used since the 1940s. In ECT, doctors anesthetize a patient and use electric current to induce a seizure that releases antidepressant neurotransmitters in the brain.

Psychiatrists say that ECT can fog short-term memory. But they also say techniques have improved considerably since the days when the treatment was so harshly portrayed in Ken Kesey's 1962 novel (and subsequent movie), *One Flew Over the Cuckoo's Nest*.

Last summer, the FDA approved vagus nerve stimulation, a treatment in which surgeons wrap a wire connected to a battery-operated pacemaker around the vagus nerve in the neck. An electrical pulse stimulates the nerve, releasing chemicals that help combat depression.

But medications don't work for everyone, and some patients are reluctant to try treatments that involve surgery and seizures. "They scare the hell out of me," Aguilar said.

Magnetic treatment offers another advantage over ECT: the patient remains awake and alert during the 40-minute process. "They can watch television, listen to an iPod or do whatever they want to do," said Peter Anastasiou, a Neuronetics spokesman.

History of TMS

TMS got its start in 1985 when English scientists wanted to see whether a magnetic field could stimulate nerves and possibly treat neurological disorders.

"We were looking for a way to maybe help people with things like carpal tunnel syndrome or multiple sclerosis," said Reza Jalinous, who was part of the original University of Sheffield team and is now a co-owner of Magstim Co. Limited, a Welsh company that sells TMS devices.

These days, a handful of firms sell TMS equipment to researchers in the United States—and to clinicians who use them to treat patients for depression in Canada, Australia and Europe, where the technique is approved.

TMS has also been the focus of dozens of studies, including a $7 million, four-year study that began last year with funding from the National Institute of Mental Health. But U.S. researchers say that the Neuronetics clinical trial is the most thorough.

Neuronetic's device is designed with a patented magnetic coil that passes a magnetic field into the prefrontal cortex, "tickling" it and easing depression, company officials say. The firm applied for FDA approval in mid-April. The agency could grant approval in the next few months or conduct an in-depth review that could take much longer.

"It won't be good for everything, but it will be good for depression and probably for a few other things," said Dr. John

O'Reardon, a psychiatrist at the University of Pennsylvania who treated Aguilar in the clinical trial but has no financial interest in Neuronetics. He has been using TMS in research for six years.

Anastasiou declined to disclose the cost of the clinical trial or the expected price tag for its Neuro-Star TMS Therapy System because, he said, FDA rules prohibit those discussions of unapproved products.

Testing the Procedure

In the clinical trial, 301 patients at 23 sites in the United States, Canada and Australia were randomly selected to receive either magnetic stimulation or a placebo treatment in which a plate blocked the magnetic field.

The volunteers were not paid and to qualify they had to be unresponsive to other depression treatments. Treatments were given Monday through Friday, up to 40 minutes a day for up to six weeks. Patients were monitored for six months, Demitrack said.

After the randomized trial was completed, all patients were allowed to receive real TMS treatments as part of an "open label" study.

In the randomized trial, 25 percent of those given TMS improved noticeably, compared with 12 percent in the placebo group, Demitrack said. In the open label study, in which patients knew they were getting TMS, about 45 percent responded.

Considering that patients in the trial had been unresponsive to other therapies, the results were impressive, according to Dr. Mark George, a TMS researcher at Medical University of South Carolina and principal investigator on the separate NIMH study.

"They showed it was safe and that it made people well," George said.

But other experts say it might be too early to design treatments that target specific areas of the brain because so little is known about its workings.

"We might be treating one signal of a disease, one side effect of it, but not the disease itself," Wassermann said.

Many of depression's biological underpinnings remain a mystery, and targeting a specific area could prove ineffective, said Dr. Ralph Hoffman, the Yale psychiatrist who did the work with schizophrenics who heard voices.

"There's little that's known about the physiology of depression. It's a real limitation," Hoffman said. Demitrack agreed that some biological roots of depression remain elusive. But he said that shouldn't stop doctors from using a new type of treatment for depression when drugs and psychotherapy don't work.

"The question is, do we know enough about the biology, the symptoms and causes of depression to test and use a new therapy? I think the answer to that is yes," he said. "The problem is that depression has multiple biological underpinnings, so there's no one therapy that will work in everybody, and I don't think TMS will work for everybody either."

CHAPTER 4

The Debate
over Antidepressants

The History
of Antidepressants

David Healy

David Healy is a former secretary of the British Association of Psychopharmacology who frequently writes on the issue of psychotropic drugs. In the following excerpt from his book Let Them Eat Prozac, *Healy traces the development of mood-elevating drugs from the earliest days of the 1920s to the present. Marketing has always been an essential part of antidepressants' and tranquilizers' popularity with both the public and the medical community, Healy writes. Drug companies are not above manipulating public fears and perceptions about "nerves" and depression in order to sell their drugs, he argues, and in fact have done so throughout the twentieth century.*

During the first eighty years of the twentieth century, depression was considered a rare disorder. The vast majority of nervous states were seen as anxiety disorders. Individuals suffering from "nerves" were noted to have increased heart rates, butterflies in their stomach or other gastrointestinal complaints, headaches, sweating, and breathlessness. The influence of Freud and psychoanalysis did a great deal to popularize the existence of nerves of this kind and to shape the portrayal of this condition as an anxiety disorder that could be treated, whether by drugs or by talking therapies.

Popular thinking was also influenced by the world wars, which brought home the idea that extreme environmental stress could produce "nervous breakdowns." The most common treatment of the condition was sedation. Opiates or alcohol had been the sedative of choice through the nineteenth century. Bromides and barbiturates replaced these in the first half of the twentieth century. In the 1930s, dexamphetamine and other stimulants were marketed for people who suffered from chronic fatigue. The first of "mother's little helpers," Dexamyl, combining a stimulant and a sedative—dexamphetamine and amylobarbitone—appeared in the 1950s, producing dramatic benefits for "nerves" that are still not easily explained.

People with "nerves" could access these treatments without much medical intervention, since most were available over the counter. Once medical help was sought, a prescription could be refilled regularly without further medical contact. As a result, it is harder to gauge the level of nervous problems in the first half of the twentieth century than now, but it is likely that it was no lower and no higher than today.

The launching of meprobamate under the brand name Miltown in 1955 was a watershed. This drug was discovered by Frank Berger, a Czechoslovak who emigrated to the United States before the Second World War. Drug discovery at that time had little input from academic medicine, and Berger was working on muscle relaxants in the laboratories of Carter-Wallace when he discovered that meprobamate calmed laboratory animals without unduly sedating them. Since muscular tension was a feature of anxiety, muscular relaxation without sedation might be good for anxiety states. Given that his new drug was less sedative than older drugs, Berger adopted a new term—*tranquilizer*.

Miltown at first looked to be the ideal answer for everyday anxiety. It produced a pleasant, relaxed feeling that "liberated" people from their nerves, encouraging them to do things they would not have done otherwise. Because it left many people feeling *better* than well, a Miltown craze was born in the newspapers and on radio and the newly emerging television.

A Tranquilizer Craze

Librium and Valium followed Miltown in the early 1960s. These benzodiazepine drugs looked as effective as Miltown but were even less likely to cause sedation or dependence. Hoffman-La Roche brilliantly marketed Librium and Valium, "helping" doctors to realize that a significant proportion of the physical complaints appearing in their offices might be manifestations of anxiety. What drove ulcers, if not anxiety? No one knew what caused hypertension, but it sounded as though these patients were bottling up their anxiety. Patients with asthma or other breathing conditions were often anxious, as were patients with headaches. For all these conditions, it became widespread practice to prescribe a tranquilizer along with whatever other medication the patient was taking. Physicians were encouraged to give Valium to college students who were facing the stresses of their new environment. Housewives were regularly prescribed Valium to cope with the stresses of new suburban lifestyles. Busy executives were taking it. Sales of Valium soared in the 1970s, until at one point it was the best-selling drug on the market.

Critics began to question the appropriateness of tranquilizing on such a mass scale. Would these new agents dull the natural competitiveness people need for survival in a hard world? Would people (and, indeed, nations) become less fit for survival if these drugs were overused? Problems coping at college surely were not *medical* disorders. The student revolutionaries of the late 1960s argued that it was the political system that was confusing and disorienting people, and the appropriate therapeutic intervention was to change the system rather than treat individuals. This general political charge took a specific shape when the British government took Roche to court on the issue of overpricing and won.

Debating Dependence

The benzodiazepine story came to an end in the 1980s. But the undoing of the benzodiazepines came not from overcharging or from mass prescribing to mask social ills. It came when the possibility was raised, around the end of the 1970s, that these drugs that had been so relied upon might lead to dependence. This specter helped create the phenomenon of health news. Before 1980, it was unusual to see health coverage in major newspapers. In the 1980s, however, stories about benzodiazepines began to appear regularly, contributing to a regular health section in newspapers. Talk shows such as *Donahue* and *Oprah* in America and *That's Life* in England, on which individuals discuss their problems, furthered these developments. Health was a natural subject for these shows, leading indirectly to the formation of coalitions of campaigning patients on matters such as benzodiazepine dependence.

The benzodiazepines were portrayed as addictive, despite protests from clinicians that this was not the case. Animal tests of abuse liability, the establishment argued, showed benzodiazepines did not have the abuse liability of heroin, cocaine, or other classic drugs of abuse. Addicts might use "Benzos," but they had little street value. In contrast, they had a clear therapeutic niche, and most patients were able to discontinue benzodiazepines without incident. The establishment views carried little weight against a rising tide of discontent and the outlining of the concept of normal dose dependence by Malcolm Lader, a professor of psychopharmacology at the Maudsley Hospital in London, and others. Before the 1980s, addicts had been socially shunned as perpetrators of their own downfall. In contrast, benzodiazepine "addicts" were seen as victims of a medico-pharmaceutical establishment, and blame was directed at medical practitioners and pharmaceutical company executives. Doctors and drug companies became the villains of the piece.

Popularity in Japan

The benzodiazepines rapidly passed in Western public perception from remarkably safe medicines to one of the greatest dangers to modern society. The extraordinary nature of this development can be seen in sharper focus when contrasted with what happened in Japan. Whether because of safer prescribing in lower doses, or because the Japanese are genetically less liable to dependence on benzodiazepines, or because the tranquilized state was more socially desirable in Japan than comparable states of mind in the West, there was never a problem with benzodiazepine use in Japan. When the tranquilizer market collapsed in the West, it continued to grow in Japan, despite medical reforms and a growing acceptance that benzodiazepines should not be prescribed for hypertension, ulcers, or similar conditions. In contrast, the Japanese antidepressant market remained a small one, with no Prozac available as late as 2003.

An important, though rarely mentioned, element in this story was the role of other pharmaceutical companies in bringing the benzodiazepines down. When concerns were first raised about the benzodiazepines, another group of drugs active on serotonin was in clinical trials. This group of drugs, of which buspirone (BuSpar) was later the best known, was in market development, and as part of this, Mead Johnson in America and Bristol-Myers Squibb in Britain were prepared to highlight the problems of the benzodiazepines as part of a campaign to market buspirone as the first non-dependence-producing anxiolytic.

Bristol-Myers Squibb sponsored symposia at conferences, special supplements in journals, and other articles by experts. They provided an opportunity for speakers to address large audiences of primary-care practitioners and psychiatrists, outlining the hazards of the benzodiazepines. This type of exercise, treading a fine line between education and marketing, is commonplace. It may do good. It may do harm. In this case it backfired. Physicians and others were skeptical of the idea of a non-dependence-producing anxiolytic. The benzodiazepine crisis had educated physicians to expect that any drug that treated anxiety would in due course be found to cause dependence. Patient resistance to BuSpar paralleled this physician skepticism: Buspirone was not as pleasant to take as the benzodiazepines. It flopped. The tranquilizer era was over, and an antidepressant era was about to start.

The Antidepressant Era

Conventionally, the antidepressant story starts in 1957 with the twin discoveries of the tricyclic antidepressant imipramine, by Roland Kuhn, and the monoamine oxidase inhibitor (MAOI) iproniazid, by Nathan Kline. But the pharmaceutical companies involved, Geigy and Roche, had little interest in an antidepressant and did nothing to promote either of these drugs. Very few clinicians in office practice seemed to encounter depression. When Merck launched another antidepressant, amitriptyline, in 1961, unlike Geigy and Roche it decided it needed to market depression as well as amitriptyline. Frank Ayd from Baltimore, the first investigator to detect the antidepressant properties of amitriptyline, had published a 1961 book titled *Recognizing the Depressed Patient*. Merck commissioned fifty thousand copies of the book to distribute to general physicians and psychiatrists wherever the compound was being marketed. Amitriptyline quickly became the best selling of this group of drugs, later called the tricyclic antidepressants (TCAs or tricyclics) because of their three-ringed molecular structure. But despite Merck's efforts, the antidepressants remained the poor cousins of the tranquilizers.

During the 1960s and 1970s, senior figures in biological psychiatry such as Nathan Kline and Fred Goodwin in the United States and Paul Kielholz in Switzerland argued that many patients diagnosed as anxious were in fact depressed, and the appropriate treatment was an antidepressant rather than an anxiolytic. This vision led Kielholz in 1972, supported by Ciba-Geigy, to set up the first meeting of the Committee for the Prevention and Treatment of Depression. The brief of the group was to establish what needed to be done to improve the recognition and treatment of depressive disorders. In the United States, Paul Wender and Don Klein set up a comparable National Foundation for Depressive Illness in the late 1980s.

Social Psychiatry and the DSM III

The research underpinning the new thinking about depression came from social psychiatrists. In 1966, Michael Shepherd in London published the first book to suggest primary-care physicians rather than psychiatrists might be seeing the vast bulk of nervous problems, and that a great many of these problems could be viewed as depression. This laid the groundwork for a host of studies in the 1980s surveying depression in the general population, which in turn formed the basis for marketing the SSRIs (selective serotonin reuptake inhibitors). Far from welcoming the marketing of the SSRIs, Shepherd regarded the consequences of his research falling into the hands of pharmaceutical companies as comparable to those of the sorcerer leaving his apprentice alone in the workshop.

Another development came with the creation of DSM-III [Diagnostic and Statistical Manual of Mental Disorders, published by the American Psychiatric Association]. Following the introduction of the new psychotropic [affecting the mind] drugs, in the late 1960s psychiatry was faced with the development of antipsychiatry, which questioned the legitimacy of psychiatric diagnoses and practices. Psychologists posing as patients famously got themselves admitted to psychiatric hospitals, unsuspected by medical staff even though real patients easily detected the fraud. The controversies swirling around psychiatry led in 1980 to the introduction of operational criteria for psychiatric disorders in a revised diagnostic manual, DSM-III. In DSM, anxiety neurosis was broken down into a number of apparently different disorders—social phobia, generalized anxiety disorder, panic disorder, post-traumatic stress disorder (PTSD), and obsessive-compulsive disorder. In contrast, the depressive disorders were collapsed into one large category—major depressive disorder.

DSM-III's new formulations emerged just as Kielholz's Committee for the Prevention and Treatment of Depression laid the basis for national campaigns such as Depression—Awareness, Recognition, and Treatment (DART), in the United States, and Defeat Depression, in the United Kingdom. Eli Lilly supported both campaigns. In the case of DART, Lilly funds went into eight million brochures titled *Depression: What You Need to Know* and two hundred thousand posters. As Lew Judd, the director of the U.S. National Institute of Mental Health (NIMH) in 1987, put it: "By making these materials on depressive illness available, accessible in physicians' offices all over the country, important information is effectively reaching the public in settings which encourage questions, discussion, treatment, or referral." Campaigns like this can do great good—or they can be self-serving.

Marketing Depression

In the early 1990s, surveys by the Defeat Depression campaign found most people thought everyday depression was not the kind of condition that should be treated with pills. But DART and other national campaigns were launched on the waves of an incoming tide. The 1980s saw a dramatic increase in articles about depression in both medical journals and general-readership magazines. Those hostile to psychiatry may smell a conspiracy, but the real interpretation has probably to do with a vacuum opening up. Both academic and lay media were reporting benzodiazepine horror stories in contrast to the feel-good stories of previous years. There was a vacancy for stories about a new feel-good drug. News that clinicians such as Nathan Kline and Fred Goodwin had been trying to cultivate for years, previously choked of light by the canopy of over hanging tranquilizer publicity, was given a chance to grow. But no one expected it would turn out quite so easy to change medical perceptions.

The depression campaigns had a twofold strategy. One was to alert physicians and third-party payers in health care to the huge economic burdens of untreated depression. The campaigns were so successful in this strategy that a decade later no one bats an eye at claims that depression is one of the greatest single health burdens on mankind. But no one asks whether treatments that are supposed to make a difference actually do produce benefits. There is plenty of evidence that antidepressants can be shown to do something in the short term but almost no evidence that things turn out better in the long run, and there are many reasons to worry that we might be making things worse. Something must surely be going wrong if the frequency of depression apparently jumps a thousandfold since the introduction of the antidepressants.

The second strategy involved a series of educational campaigns to show physicians how many cases of depression they were missing—to shame them into detecting and treating depression. The tragedy of Sylvia Plath's suicide, for instance, was held up as something that could have been prevented with better recognition of depression. This new emphasis has almost certainly led to diagnosis of depression for many people who do not regard themselves as being depressed or in need of treatment. In individual cases, this heightening of clinician sensitivity to depression may have saved lives; on a broader front, there is no evidence that mass detection and treatment of depression have lowered national suicide or disability rates.

Problem of the Antidepressant Delay

The antidepressant story has a further important twist. The conventional wisdom as of the early 1980s was that, unlike tranquilizers, which were feel-good agents that delivered a relatively immediate payoff, antidepressants took several weeks to work. Prescribers were educated to tell patients they could even expect to feel worse for some weeks before they began to feel better. This strategy sent the message that these were not quick-fix pills but rather medications that really corrected the problem.

But this educational information becomes problematic when these drugs are made available on prescription only from physicians trained to deliver just this message. Against a background of instructions that these pills might take many weeks to work, on the one hand, for many doctors the idea that Prozac or other antidepressants might lead to suicidal tendencies or other severe problems during the early period "before the pills begin working" seems a contradiction in terms. On the other hand, patients faced with a doctor who has not been educated about the potential hazards in the early phase of treatment risk being trapped by their relationship with their doctor. Where patients would probably discontinue an over-the-counter medication if it did not seem to suit them, regard for their doctor, who very likely will advise them to continue treatment, can convince many to continue with a treatment that might kill them.

The messages of the depression campaigns were based on treatment of people hospitalized for the types of severe depression described by [writer and psychologist] Kay Redfield Jamison. For these depressions, it made sense to avoid recurrences, and long-term treatment seemed a good idea. But this was an entirely different kind of disorder from the stress and adjustment reactions and adolescent turmoil for which the SSRIs increasingly came to be administered in the 1990s, disorders that last on average less than three months. Furthermore, the economics of depression put forward to justify mass detection and treatment of depression were all worked out initially on the basis of the Jamison form of depression. None of the assumptions of such models—for example, that treatment will lower suicide rates or improve quality of life—holds for the kinds of "depression" that exist in the wider society.

Current Antidepressants Are Flawed but Needed

Apoorva Mandavilli

In the following article from the journal Nature Medicine, *senior news editor Apoorva Mandavilli analyzes the safety and efficacy of the current group of antidepressants, SSRIs. The drugs have provided undeniable relief for millions suffering from depression but they are far from perfect. In fact, she writes, SSRIs have been suspected of increasing the risk of suicide in teenagers and possibly adults. Most experts agree that a safer depression drug would be preferable, Mandavilli explains, but a better chemical alternative has yet to be found. However, antidepressants are an extremely profitable business for the pharmaceutical companies, giving them a strong impetus to advance the research in that field. Meanwhile, Mandavilli writes, patients would do well to use current antidepressants with caution.*

In 1988, Julio Licinio was finishing his residency in psychiatry at the New York Hospital-Cornell Medical Center. In those days, the mainstay of treatment for patients with depression was a class of drugs called tricyclics. The drugs caused serious side effects and the risk of a fatal overdose, so patients were closely monitored.

That year, the US Food and Drug Administration (FDA) approved fluoxetine, a selective serotonin reuptake inhibitor, or SSRI, for depression. Marketed by Eli Lilly as Prozac, fluoxetine rapidly gained a reputation for being as effective as tricyclics, but safer and with fewer side effects. Within a year, sales of Prozac rocketed to $350 million. "It was a big turning point," says Licinio, now a professor of psychiatry at the University of California in Los Angeles.

"The risk of suicide seems if anything to increase with anti-depressants."

David Healy, North Wales department of psychological medicine.

Within just a few years, Prozac, and others like it that followed, transformed the way antidepressants were prescribed. "Tricyclics were not prescribed like candy, nobody would write a month's supply of tricyclics and send the patient away," Licinio says. But because SSRIs are safe in terms of overdose, he says, "People think of them as safe overall."

But that might change: in recent months [Since late 2003], the UK has banned the use of most SSRIs in those under 18 and the FDA is meeting on September 13 and 14 [2004] to review the link betweem the drugs and suicide in adolescents. Editor's Note: The FDA has permitted use of SSRIs for teenagers but required the drugs to carry a warning box noting the link. Although most of the controversy surrounds the drugs' use in children, there is renewed attention on whether they are safe even in adults.

If new analysis finds that SSRIs and other drugs of its class are unsafe, what are the alternatives? Pharmaceutical pipelines for antidepressants are discouragingly dry. What's more, any new drug for depression might carry the same risk of suicide—unless pharmaceutical companies can design one that would rapidly lift melancholic moods, says Licinio. "But such a drug doesn't exist."

Severe depression is often characterized by suicidal impulses but most patients are so lacking in energy and paralyzed by their illness—a condition dubbed 'psychomotor retardation'—that they don't act on those impulses. But when patients are treated with antidepressants, different symptoms of the illness lift at different rates. "The psychomotor retardation is the first thing to go, existential sadness is the last thing to go," says Licinio.

Psychiatrists recognize that, by giving people the energy to act out their destructive thoughts, the drugs effectively make people acutely vulnerable to suicide. But family physicians and internists, who have increasingly taken on the treatment of depressed patients, might not know that. "Treatment of depression has this built-in period when people become more suicidal before they get better—we were all taught this," says Licinio. "That never went away, people just forgot about it."

Mysteries of the Mind

"If anything, SSRIs lower the risk of suicide statistically."

Phil Skolnick, DOV Pharmaceuticals.

A safe and effective drug for depression would be a goldmine for any pharmaceutical company. Depression affects about one in ten people and some studies estimate that one in five women might at one point in life battle a depressive episode. That's not all: SSRIs are prescribed 'off label' for any number of conditions, from anxiety and obsessive-compulsive disorders to premenstrual dysphoric disorder and addictions—including shopping addiction. Because of the drug's effect in delaying orgasm, it has also been prescribed for premature ejaculation. Worldwide, the market for antidepressants is an estimated $17 billion.

But for decades, every new contender for that market has been just a slight variation on its predecessors, in large part because no one really knows what depression is or what causes it.

We know, for instance, that depression has a familial or genetic component, that it is attributable in part to life events, particularly those that occur early in life, and that it is accompanied by high levels of stress hormones and anhedonia—a lack of enjoyment in food, sex and other pleasurable things. Beyond that, the details are sketchy.

With only a tenuous grasp on the workings of the depressed mind, scientists have been hard-pressed to find drugs to treat it. "All the molecular targets we point to seem to be linked somehow to the symptoms," says David Schulz, executive director for CNS [Central Nervous System] Discovery Biology and General Pharmacology at Pfizer. "We have no convincing evidence at all that [the existing drugs] contribute to the underlying pathology."

In fact, the current repertoire of drugs is largely a result of luck. The first antidepressants were discovered in the 1950s when people being treated for tuberculosis reported feeling happier and more energetic. Scientists later found that the drugs increase the levels of a group of chemicals called monoamines that transmit messages across nerve cells. Existing antidepressants work either by preventing the breakdown or by inhibiting the reuptake of these monoamines—serotonin, norepinephrine and dopamine—from the synapse.

Tricyclics nonselectively raise levels of serotonin and norepinephrine. Most new drugs are selective for serotonin, and a few—such as reboxetine, marketed as Edronax in Europe—target norepinephrine. Some of the drugs increase appetite, others have a sedative component, yet others dramatically boost energy levels. Because different people respond to different drugs, experts say it is important to have so many variations on the same theme. But overall, differences in the drugs are marginal.

At the level of neurons, the drugs' action is seen within hours, but full clinical effect can take up to eight weeks. "What that tells us is that all the drugs we have are acting so remote from the mechanism that produces the antidepressant effect," says Florian Holsboer, director of the Max Planck Institute of Psychiatry in Munich [Germany]. "So there must be something else in between."

To tap more closely into the basic underpinnings of depression, companies are exploring targets in stress-hormone regulation, brain-specific proteins and circadian rhythms. For instance, about 75% of Wyeth Pharmaceuticals' programs in depression and anxiety focus on new mechanisms. But drugs that rely on new mechanisms are in the very initial stages of being tested. For the time being, monoamines continue to be the primary targets.

Is More Better?

Approved this summer [2004], Eli Lilly's Cymbalta exemplifies a new trend in antidepressant development. Like tricyclics, Cymbalta raises levels of both serotonin and norepinephrine. GlaxoSmithKline's (GSK) Wellbutrin XL, approved in 2003, affects norepinephrine and dopamine. In early August [2004], DOV Pharmaceuticals licensed two triple reuptake inhibitors—which target all three monoamines—to Merck. Another triple reuptake compound at DOV is set to enter trials later this year [2004].

The rationale is that by aiming at multiple receptors, the drugs will either be faster or capture a bigger percent of responders, says Phil Skolnick, chief scientific officer of DOV Pharmaceuticals.

But critics say that the combination drugs are a marketing ploy. "[The theories] are so speculative and they're presented with so much authority," says Jon Jureidini, head of psychological medicine at Women's and Children's Hospital in Adelaide, Australia. When SSRIs first emerged, the companies defined depression as imbalances in serotonin, Jureidini notes. "Now that they're promoting the serotonin [plus] norepinephrine drugs, it's not just all about serotonin anymore. It's about other neurotransmitters," he says. "The science follows the marketing to a certain extent."

Jureidini and others say there is no evidence that the double reuptake drugs are any better. In fact, the FDA's analysis cites the highest number of problems with venlafaxine (Effexor), which raises levels of both serotonin and norepinephrine.

Experts outside the industry are more optimistic about antagonists of the corticotropin releasing factor (CRF), a stress hormone. The link between stress and depression is well-documented and there is evidence that levels of cortisol are elevated in the spinal fluid of depressed patients. "That's probably the best biology that's been worked out for depression," says Ranga Krishnan, chair of psychiatry at Duke University.

The only human trial of a CRF antagonist was a small but promising proof-of-principle study by Holsboer's group in Munich. But at high doses, the compound produced a troubling increase in liver enzymes, and was shelved when Belgium-based Janssen, which held the license, was acquired by Johnson and Johnson (J & J).

In 1996, Pfizer also abandoned a CRF antagonist when researchers there uncovered toxicity in preclinical studies. Still, both Holsboer and Pfizer maintain that the problems were specific to those compounds and have no bearing on the validity of the hypothesis. Nearly every major company is now pursuing CRF antagonists, which are widely acknowledged as the lead alternative to available antidepressants.

Most of the CRF compounds are in phase 1 trials or earlier. Because cortisol regulates immune response to infections, a successful CRF antagonist would have to act on the brain receptors but not in the periphery. "That's not an easy task," notes Krishnan. As a result, he says, "everyone is going very, very slowly and making sure they understand the pharmacology."

Lower on the list of candidate drugs are those that target substance P, a member of the nuerokinin family of brain-specific peptides. Merck's report in 1998 that its substance P antagonist was a powerful antidepressant marked the first promising results from a non-monoamine drug. But in subsequent phase 3 trials, the drug proved ineffective. It is now being marketed for nausea associated with chemotherapy.

Merck, Pfizer and others have since shelved their substance P programs, but a few companies, including GSK, continue to pursue them. Other drugs in early development target receptors for the neurotransmitter glutamate, or attempt to reset the disrupted sleep patterns in depressed patients.

Trial and Error

The biggest hurdle in developing drugs that veer from the monoamine hypothesis is that there are few animal models to validate them. The scarcity of models is a catch-22 [a no-win situation] of sorts: depression is considered a state unique to human beings, meaning animals do not get depressed, so animal models can only reflect pieces of the symptoms or behavior.

Most existing models recreate monoamine defects and may not be predictive for the new classes of compounds. But that's not likely to stop the companies. "If we failed to see activity, we wouldn't be discouraged by it," says Pfizer's Schulz. "If you believe strongly in your hypothesis and there's a lot of science behind it, you should go ahead anyway."

Once in human trials, the compounds are up against a formidable 'placebo effect,' which dominates discussions about antidepressant development. Some studies say that in as many as half of all depression trials, the drugs do not prove significantly better than a placebo. Critics argue that this is because the drugs are no better than placebos. But many experts—including those without financial ties to the industry—say the placebo effect is a real challenge.

Depression is often defined by arbitrary and subjective symptoms rather than concrete physiological data, so the kind of people recruited into trials can vary wildly. Companies also shy away from the severely depressed and increasingly enroll those with mild or transient depression, the very group most likely to respond to placebos.

Future trials are also likely to be scrutinized carefully for any link between the drug and suicide. One analysis by David Healy, director of the North Wales department of psychological medicine [in the UK], suggests that in mildly depressed or anxious people and even among healthy individuals, the drugs can trigger suicidal thoughts. "The risk of suicide seems if anything to increase with antidepressants," says Healy, who has consulted for many manufacturers.

But Healy's analysis is hotly debated. Some, like Licinio—who has no ties to manufacturers of antidepressants—say the risk is inherent to treating depression. Others say most suicides are by people who are not on antidepressants. "If anything, SSRIs lower the risk of suicide statistically," says DOV's Skolnick.

But most agree that much more needs to be done to understand exactly how the drugs affect depressed brains. "I don't dispute the numbers. What I don't accept from [Healy's] analysis is that there is a direct causal link," says Spilios Argyropoulos, consultant psychiatrist at South London and Maudsley NHS Trust [in England]. "It's not a straightforward question and it's not as straightforward an answer as it's made to be."

Gray Skies Ahead:

There is almost universal agreement among experts that antidepressants are overused and oversold. But even the most skeptical of critics agree that the drugs are sorely needed. "I'm in favor of using these drugs but I think in the case of the people less severely ill, you've got to take much, much more care," says Healy.

Pushing the drugs too hard, too fast, without enough information about their safety, can eventually bring on too many restrictions—and keep them from the people who really need them, Healy says. Lawsuits from various governments are pressuring companies to be more forthcoming about negative results from trials so that people can be aware of the risks long before there is a crisis. GSK has released results from its trials on its website. Merck and J & J have both supported the idea of a clinical trial registry and Eli Lilly has said it would list all trials for its approved drugs by the end of the year.

But it is not clear how much of a difference that will make. Lilly's pledge only applies to its approved drugs: any unpublished information about earlier-stage drugs has to be cleared through a lengthy approval process. Merck will not disclose information on any drugs before they enter phase 3 trials [the second-to-last phase of testing].

Still, the controversy is likely to change the way the industry operates. "The way it's affecting us is that we're a little more conservative in launching trials in the first place," says Schulz. "The days when we throw a lot of money at depression and hope for the best are probably over."

Realistically, companies will also have to abandon their hope of developing a drug that will work in all people, says Holsboer, who predicts that future antidepressants will be targeted to specific subgroups of patients. Holsboer, Licinio and others are trying to find genetic variations that might predict whether someone will respond to a given antidepressant. Others are hunting for genes that might predispose people to depression.

In the meantime, people might begin to think twice before popping the pills, and consider opting instead for psychotherapy. Physicians might also exercise much more caution before prescribing the drugs, says Licinio. "At least this will alert people that this is not cosmetic psychopharmacology," he says. "You have to follow the patients."

Antidepressants' Link to Adolescent Suicide

Jennifer Barrett Ozols

In the following article, author Jennifer Barrett Ozols explores findings that link antidepressant use to increased rates of suicide in children and adolescents. Instances of teenagers killing themselves soon after being placed on the drugs have led the FDA to impose their strongest warning on antidepressant packaging, Ozols writes. Researchers do not fully understand why this link exists, except to note that teenagers' brains are still developing in ways that adult brains are not. Antidepressants still help far more than they harm, the author notes. But their use in adolescents will have to be more carefully monitored. Jennifer Barrett Ozols writes about religion, politics, and health, among other topics, for Newsweek.

The Woodwards will never know for sure if their daughter committed suicide [in 2003] because of an adverse reaction to an antidepressant. But Tom Woodward is convinced that if he had known then about the increased risk of suicide in some young patients, it could have saved their 17-year-old's life. "If we had been given that information in advance, I know Julie would still be here," he says.

Julie Woodward took her life in the summer of 2003. When her parents—and others whose children had killed themselves after starting to take antidepressants—began raising questions about the deaths, their concerns helped to prompt the Food and Drug Administration (FDA) to re-examine pharmaceutical companies' clinical trial data on antidepressants and adolescents this year. It found that, overall, children using antidepressants were nearly twice as likely to have suicidal tendencies than depressed children taking placebos. The agency announced [in October 2004] that the risk was sufficient to require a "black box" warning label on all antidepressants. A black-box label is the government's strongest measure short of banning the drugs. The warning label describes the increased risk of suicidal thoughts and behavior in children and adolescents on antidepressant medications and notes what uses the drugs have been approved or not approved for in these patients. (Prozac is currently the only medication approved to treat depression in children and adolescents.) The FDA is also developing a patient medication guide listing the risks and precautions that will be distributed by pharmacists to patients taking the drugs.

Childrens' Brains vs. Adult Brains

The next question: do adults on antidepressants face similar risks? On that, the jury's still out. "The child's brain is at a different developmental stage than an adult's, so you expect a different response in antidepressants, whether it's less improvement or worse or different side effects," says Dr. Wayne K. Goodman, who chaired the joint meeting of two federal advisory panels that called for the black-box warnings for children and teenagers. "But what's to say that there is something magic about being 18 versus 19 years old? What is the boundary between a child and an adult?"

That problem was underscored in February when one of the "healthy" adult participants—a 19-year-old bible-school student—hanged herself while enrolled in a clinical trial for Eli Lilly and Company's new antidepressant, Cymbalta. The FDA has since approved Cymbalta to treat depression and diabetes-related pain. Lilly pointed out that the drug, which increases serotonin and norepinephrine levels in the brain, was tested with more than 6,000 depressed adults worldwide,-

and was found to be "safe and effective" overall in clinical trials. (The company didn't study the safety or efficacy of Cymbalta in children.)

[In September 2004], the FDA announced plans to re-examine clinical trial data for thousands of depressed adults as well to see if there's evidence that any suffered increased suicidal thoughts and behaviors while taking antidepressants. Most of the antidepressant drugs commonly used today—including Prozac, Zoloft, Paxil and Celexa—belong to a group called selective serotonin reuptake inhibitors (or SSRIs). They work by influencing levels of serotonin, the neurotransmitter that helps control moods in the brain. Others, like Serzone and Wellbutrin, target multiple receptors in the brain.

"These are serious medicines and should probably only be prescribed by practitioners willing to do the follow-up with patients and monitor them as closely as they need to be monitored," cautions Dr. Sandra Kweder, deputy director of the Office of New Drugs at the FDA's Center for Drug Evaluation and Research. "The risk isn't large and, by far, these medicines have helped people orders of magnitude beyond the harm they may have done. But no medicine is without risks—none."

Protecting Patients

Even before its black-box decision, the FDA earlier this year asked the makers of 10 leading antidepressants to include labels alerting both doctors and consumers to danger signs like agitation, anxiety or hostility in patients of all ages. But critics say such warnings can get lost in the fine print.

"Any severe risk should be spelled out," says Vera Hassner Sharav, president of the Alliance for Human Research Protection, a patients' rights organization. "People have a right to know. We're not going to scare people off with a warning. It's just to help them make a thoughtful decision—not an impetuous one based on advertising."

Kweder says the agency will not consider requiring the same black-box warnings for adults until it has re-evaluated the data for dozens of trials. That process is expected to take much longer than the examination of data for under-18s because there are more studies involving adults. "It could last easily a year, if not longer," she says. "It's a much, much bigger undertaking."

The FDA first investigated reports of suicide among adult antidepressant users when Prozac began to be widely used in the early 1990s. "I was hoping they would have done it [required the warning] then, but they weren't recognizing the problem," says Dr. Martin Teicher, director of the laboratory of developmental psychopharmacology at McLean Hospital in Belmont, Mass. In early 1990, Teicher authored a study published in the *American Journal of Psychiatry* describing the emergence of violent suicidal thoughts in six adults taking Prozac. Teicher's report spurred a series of stories—and lawsuits—questioning whether the popular antidepressant was to blame for some patient suicides. But the FDA concluded that there was not sufficient evidence of a link between the two.

Since then, however, practitioners have noted increased "suicidality" (defined as suicidal thoughts or behavior) in a small number of adult patients after starting an antidepressant or altering the dosage. "They tamper with the brain's chemistry in ways we don't fully understand and may be at times dangerous," says Dr. Joseph Glenmullen, a Harvard psychiatrist. "While antidepressants work in a lot of people and help a lot of people, they are very harmful to others."

Adverse Responses

Glenmullen wrote the critical 2001 book *Prozac Backlash* after observing the side effects in some of his own patients in the mid-1990s. More recently, he's investigated the risks of starting antidepressants and altering dosages for his next book, *The Antidepressant Solution: The Only Step-by-Step Guide to*

Safely Overcoming Antidepressant Withdrawal, Dependence, and Addiction due out early [in 2005]. While he agrees there are differences between the brains of children and adults, Glenmullen dismisses claims that the risks of suicidality are limited to children as "industry spin" based on "junk science."

Teicher, who is now studying how depression affects the brains of patients between 18 and 22 years old, says tremendous changes in the brain do occur during childhood and early adolescence that may make younger patients more "sensitive" to the medication. Still, he says that adults are likely to face similar risks to children.

While only a small percentage might wind up with a significant adverse response, both the FDA and psychiatrists agree that all patients should be monitored closely as soon as they begin taking the antidepressants. "There has been this mistake of saying, 'Oh, it takes three to four weeks for it to work, so give the patients the pills and have them come back three to four weeks later,' which is really dangerous," says Teicher.

Researchers now consider the first two weeks the riskiest time period for patients who experience adverse side effects. The Woodwards say their daughter, Julie, began acting strangely almost immediately after she started taking Zoloft—unexpectedly pushing her mother one afternoon, gnawing nervously on a napkin at the kitchen table and pacing the floors. But when her parents called the clinic that dispensed the drug, they were told not to worry because it would take a little while for Julie to adjust. Seven days after she started taking Zoloft, Julie hanged herself. "We were lulled into a false sense of security. It was devastating. She had no history of self-harm or suicide. The police went through her journals and found no reference to suicide," says Woodward, who still lives in North Wales, Pa., with his wife and three other children. "I don't want what happened to our daughter to happen to anyone else."

That may be wishful thinking. But alerting both adults and children to the warning signs can only be a step in the right direction.

Controversy over Medicating Depression

Peter D. Kramer

Peter D. Kramer is a psychiatrist and author who has written extensively on the subject of antidepressants and culture, including the books Listening to Prozac *and* Against Depression. *He is also a professor at Brown University. In the following essay, Kramer explores the link between depression and art and uses as a comparison the link between bodily disease and art. Before diseases such as epilepsy and tuberculosis were well known, Kramer writes, they were often valorized for their perceived connection to creativity. Yet, once the diseases became better known and treatments were available, this romanticizing disappeared. Depression, according to Kramer, may follow a similar path. Antidepressants are available to alleviate the symptoms, yet some wonder if that will dampen artists' creativity. However, as depression becomes better understood as an illness, rather than a state of mind, Kramer writes, this concern will most likely disappear.*

FOR 10 YEARS OR LONGER, my week-day routine as a psychiatrist had been constant: write mornings, see patients afternoons. With the publication of my book *Listening to Prozac* in 1993, new elements were added: travel and public appearances.

One question followed me from lecture to lecture, from talk show to talk show, bookstore to bookstore. Because the question was so automatic, so predictable, it took me months to appreciate how peculiar it was.

At a book signing, I might give a short introduction to this or that aspect of *Listening to Prozac*, discussing workplace

Peter D. Kramer, "The Neurotic Artist: Romanticizing Depression," *Chronicle of Higher Education*, vol. 51, May 6, 2005. Copyright © 2005 Peter D. Kramer. Reproduced in North America and the rest of the world by permission of Penguin Putnam, Inc. In the UK by permission of the author via Darnhansoff Verrill Feldman Literary Agents.

pressures to remain upbeat, say, and the ethics of using medi-cations in response. What I spoke about seemed not to matter. Inevitably someone would ask: "What if so-and-so had taken Prozac?" The candidates for drug treatment were drawn from a short roster of tortured 19th-century artists and writers. Friedrich Nietzsche and Edgar Allan Poe made frequent ap-pearances.

My response was perfunctory—a quick review of theories of art and neurosis. I resented the joking distraction from is-sues I had raised. I did not treat the what if question as I did others. I did not attend to it, puzzle over it, take it to heart.

And then one day I did. The setting was a professional meeting in Copenhagen, in 1995.

At home, as the Prozac book's popularity grew, my stand-ing among my colleagues fell—or so I feared. With a few thousand copies sold, a man is all right. With hundreds of thousands of sales, it is another matter. I was a popularizer, an opportunist who had made his way on the backs of others, the real researchers. This apprehension was a matter of hyper-sensitivity, of mild paranoia—although when a book succeeds, there are always belated "debunking" reviews, to feed an author's insecurity. Speaking invitations poured in, and still I thought I heard snickering from the back row.

But in Scandinavia! There I was a prophet with honor, like Jerry Lewis in France. The Finns were among the first to trans-late *Listening to Prozac*. Now it was being put into Swedish, with an introduction by the most eminent biological psychia-trist in Northern Europe, Marie Åsgard. The Swedes had per-suaded the Scandinavian Society for Psychopharmacology to invite me as the keynote speaker at their annual meeting.

My hosts had proposed the topic "Myths and Realities" about antidepressants. The core of the talk would concern an orthodoxy I considered mythical, the one that said antidepressants treat only depression. I wanted to review evidence that the drugs might influence personality traits in people with no mental illness at all.

I spent a pleasant afternoon in Copenhagen on my own. The morning of my presentation arrived. I was in serious company—laboratory and clinical researchers. The practicing doctors had seen effects similar to the ones I had described in my book, dramatic responses to medication. I felt myself on solid ground, the honored guest.

I launched into my talk. The audience was attentive, applause polite. A hearty fellow stood up to ask the first question. He had a smile that was familiar to me, from other audiences. His question was: "So, Dr. Kramer, what would have happened if Kierkegaard had taken Prozac?"

OF COURSE, in Copenhagen the suffering artist would be Søren Kierkegaard. Who else? He is the most famous Dane, give or take Hans Christian Andersen. Certainly Kierkegaard is the Dane best known for his melancholy, if you understand Hamlet to be fiction. Danes know Kierkegaard the way we know Mark Twain or Henry David Thoreau—perhaps more intimately. I was once told that when Danish children are sullen, parents will scold them, "Don't be such a Søren!"

Kierkegaard is part of what had brought me to Copenhagen, what had made the invitation appealing. I read Kierkegaard when I was young. My college roommate and I plowed through *Either/Or* together, after my roommate's mother died. She had lived with Hodgkin's disease for almost the whole of her son's life and had never told him, for fear of blighting his childhood. That was like something out of Kierkegaard—self-sacrifice so radical as to be disturbing.

On the flight across the Atlantic, I had browsed in a paperback version of Kierkegaard's *Diaries*. How grim they are. Kierkegaard describes self-loathing, pessimism, dread, isolation, guilt, and anomie. He writes of wanting to shoot himself. Kierkegaard complains of a "primitive melancholy . . . a huge dowry of distress." He writes, "My whole past life was in any case so altogether cloaked in the darkest melancholy, and in the most profoundly brooding of misery's fogs, that it is no wonder I was as I was." And then: "How terrible to have to buy each day, each hour—and the price varies so!" And again: "The sad thing with me is that the crumb of joy and reassurance I slowly distill in the painstakingly dyspeptic process of my thought-life I use up straightaway in just one despairing step."

On my arrival in Copenhagen, I had taken a walk to the Kierkegaard statue, in the garden of the Danish Royal Library. For good measure, I sought out Kierkegaard's grave in the old central churchyard. The walks gave time and occasion to take the measure of the man. So when I heard Kierkegaard in the usual question, I was aware of a particular person. What if effective treatment had been available to this man, the one who pays a terrible price for each day and each hour?

That was how, standing before a group of friendly faces in a standard hotel conference room, I caught a glimmer of the problem with the what if challenge: The question had nothing to do with my talk and not much to do with my book. I had asked my listeners to consider medication's effects on people who meet no criteria for any illness. How did that presentation suggest Kierkegaard?

Addressing my European colleagues, I found myself cutting short the stump speech about the neurotic artist. I restarted at a slower pace, considering the ubiquity of the what if question. We pose it automatically—but why? Do we have qualms about treating or preventing depression? It is fine to debate "cosmetic psychopharmacology"—my term for the effort to sculpt normal personality with medication. But for as long as psychiatry has been a profession, its aim has been to conquer mental illness. The what if question, the Kierkegaard question, expresses unease with the psychiatric enterprise, with the life projects of Scandinavian psychopharmacologists.

As I spoke, I wondered why the familiar taunt had never before struck me as unusual. What was depression to me, if I could hear the what if question dozens of times before finding it strange?

THERE (which is to say nowhere) the matter might have stood but for a change in the weather. A colleague had invited me for a stay at a family castle in Jutland, Denmark's more rural peninsula. But a storm grounded the ferry, so we settled instead for the usual automobile tour of Zealand, a well-traveled loop of castles and museums.

On the way back to Copenhagen, we stopped at the Isak Dinesen homestead. Dinesen, the master short-story writer and diarist, is another Danish icon—all the more since the appearance of the film version of *Out of Africa*, based on her accounts of her early married life. I had read Dinesen's work, too, in my teens. I had been taken with the ominous fables. To my family, driven from Nazi Germany, the Old World had two simultaneous meanings, high culture and cruelty. The Dinesen stories captured both.

Here we were now, my pharmacologist host and I, walking the grounds of Rungstedlund, Dinesen's farm on the North Sea. My colleague and I were discussing Dinesen's ailments, her recurrent stomach pain and leg weakness. I assumed, as Dinesen had in her lifetime, that the symptoms were late effects of the syphilis she contracted in the first year of her marriage to the feckless Baron Bror Blixen. "What," I asked my host, "if penicillin had been around in Dinesen's day?"

My question was by way of teasing—making light of any annoyance I had betrayed at the conference. The joke (if there was one) was that there was and could be no Dinesen question. Of course, if penicillin had been available in 1915, doctors would have prescribed it. No one would withhold an antibiotic from a wife innocently infected by her husband. Indeed, no one withholds antibiotics from anyone infected in any manner. No moral dilemma attaches to their use. Antibiotics' purpose, to lessen the burden of disease caused by bacteria, is unexceptionable.

It is possible to wonder whether Dinesen would have written differently if she had suffered less. Syphilis has shaped our cultural heritage. Gauguin painted his greatest canvases when he was dying of syphilis, in pain and acutely aware of his mortality. The diagnosis has occasionally been disputed, but for more than a hundred years experts have asserted that much of Nietzsche's work was composed while he suffered a mental illness, one caused by the form of syphilis that damages the brain. Still, we have no moral or aesthetic ambivalence about penicillin. We have lived with penicillin for half a century, and no one considers the world of art or ideas to be shallower, at least not for that reason.

Infectious disease can be idealized. Tuberculosis once had romantic overtones. Susan Sontag traced the form of that fantasy in her famous essay, "Illness as Metaphor." TB was a disease of recklessness, longing, sensuality, serenity, decadence, sensitivity, glamour, resignation, instinct, and instinctual renunciation, that is to say, of passion or passion repressed, but in any case a disease of emotionally enhanced or refined creatures. Sontag quotes a passage in *The Magic Mountain* where a character holds that "disease is only love transformed."

The cachet attaching to consumption diminished as science clarified the cause of the illness, and as treatment became first possible and then routine. Still, as Sontag points out, there was a lag; scientific explanation did not trump metaphor in any quick or simple manner. When the fashion finally changed, it did so with a vengeance. Tuberculosis became repulsive before it became unremarkable, one pneumonia among many. By and large, we take syphilis this way, merely as infection. Certainly we are neutral about residual manifestations, treated syphilis that shows itself as leg or stomach pain. If syphilis has moral or metaphorical overtones, they are not outsize—at the least, they are in remission. That is why there is no Dinesen question.

In fact, Dinesen may have suffered not from any sequel of infection but from heavy metal poisoning—she treated her syphilis with arsenic and mercury. Or she may have been hypochondriacal and depressed. If this assumption were commonplace, it would put Dinesen in the same category as Kierkegaard—the depressed creative genius. And then lecturegoers would ask, "What if Prozac had been available in Dinesen's day?" There would be a Dinesen question after all.

This contrast—no question in the face of infectious disease, but a routine question in the face of mood disorder—implies a special status for depression. Why? If both illnesses cause the sort of suffering that can alter worldviews or shape art, why do we react to depression and syphilis differently?

AFTER THE TRIP TO DENMARK, I paid closer attention to my audience's beliefs about the nature of depression. If someone posed the what if challenge, I would ask what he had in mind. Often, it seemed, the questioner believed that the amelioration of depression might cloud a person's moral clarity or dampen a divine spark. By this account, depression has a sacred aspect.

In *Listening to Prozac*, I had worried over the use of medication in healthy people to alter personality traits like shyness. Now these concerns were being extended to cover antidepressants' intended recipients, those suffering from mental illness. The questioners seemed to understand mood disorder as a heavy dose of the artistic temperament, so that the symptoms of depression are merely personality traits and any application of antidepressants is finally cosmetic.

One confounding concern had to do with depression as a source of creativity. Why is depression different, less than fully worthy of decisive treatment? Is a link to art enough to alter the way we think about a syndrome—to move it from straightforward disease to disease-in-a-manner-of-speaking?

Sometimes I ask my audience to consider epilepsy, the set of disorders characterized by seizures, sometimes alternating with a variety of mental auras and intense experiences of emotion. Chronically, between attacks, patients with a subtype of epilepsy can be afflicted with hypergraphia, the tendency to write compulsively and at length. They may also display a characteristic personality style, one that includes intense enthusiasms, often religious fervor, and an alternation between aggression and emotional clinginess. Dostoyevsky, Flaubert, Tennyson, Swinburne, Byron, de Maupassant, Moliére, Pascal, and even Petrarch and Dante have been named as presumptively epileptic in one or another medical treatise. Poe's name often makes the list.

Epilepsy is another sacred affliction or was once. And there are medications—anticonvulsants—used to prevent or manage epilepsy. But you might give a dozen talks about quirky uses of anticonvulsants and not hear a single joking question about an artist. The vividness of the pathology and the consequent solidity of epilepsy's status as a disease cast their shadows over attempts at humor. To withhold treatment would be cruel. In the context of seizure disorders, a what if question, if asked, might point to the ironies of medical practice—how necessary interventions have unknowable consequences. But the question would not be funny. To put the matter differently: While we are protective of depression, we would be happy to eradicate epilepsy.

For me, the what if question led directly to another: What would it be like for depression to go through the transformation experienced by tuberculosis? Depression might be on the verge of that metamorphosis, from romanticized affliction into ordinary disease. Hard-to-ignore evidence was accumulating, about the bodily harm depression causes, and about the brain pathology that underlies its symptoms. Increasingly, the prevailing scientific myth had it that depression is neither more nor less than illness, but illness merely. I wanted to imagine how our beliefs, our art, our sense of self might change as the medical view became a cultural commonplace.

But I had no illusion that the moment was at hand. My work with patients and my conversations with readers reminded me daily that we retain a confused—partial, anachronistic—understanding of depression.

Organizations to Contact

The editors have compiled the following list of organizations concerned with the issues debated in this book. The descriptions are derived from materials provided by the organizations. All have publications or information available for interested readers. The list was compiled on the date of publication of the present volume; the information provided here may change. Be aware that many organizations take several weeks or longer to respond to inquiries, so allow as much time as possible.

American Academy of Child and Adolescent Psychiatry

3615 Wisconsin Ave. NW, Washington, DC   20016
(202) 966–7300 • fax: (202) 966–2891
Web site: www.accap.org

AACAP is a nonprofit organization that supports and advances child and adolescent psychiatry through research and the distribution of information. The group's goal is to remove the stigma associated with mental illness, including depression, and to assure proper treatment for minors who suffer from mental disorders. The AACAP publishes the monthly *Journal of the American Academy of Child and Adolescent Psychiatry.*

American Association of Suicidology

5221 Wisconsin Ave. NW, Washington, DC   20015
(202) 237–2280 • fax: (202) 237–2282
e-mail: info@suicidology.org
Web site: www.suicidology.org

This nonprofit education organization's mission is to understand and prevent suicide through research and public awareness programs. Founded in 1968, it provides educational opportunities for both mental health professionals and laypeople and serves as a clearinghouse for general suicide information.

The AAS publishes a journal for professionals, *Suicide and Life-Threatening Behavior,* a newsletter for members, *Newslink,* and a newsletter for suicide survivors, *Surviving Suicide.*

American Psychiatric Association
1000 Wilson Blvd., Ste. 1825, Arlington, VA   22209
(703) 907–7300
e-mail: apa@psych.org
Web site: www.psych.org

An organization of psychiatrists dedicated to studying the nature, treatment, and prevention of mental disorders, the APA helps create mental health policies, distributes information about psychiatry, and promotes psychiatric research and education. It publishes the *American Journal of Psychiatry* monthly as well as fact sheets on mental disorders that include depression.

American Psychological Association
750 First St. NE, Washington, DC   20002
(202) 336–5500 • fax (202) 336–5708
e-mail: public.affairs@apa.org
Web site: www.apa.org

The APA is the largest scientific and professional organization representing psychology in the United States and is the world's largest association of psychologists. It publishes numerous books, journals, and videos, including the monthly newspaper *APA Monitor* and the journal *American Psychologist.*

Citizens Commission on Human Rights
6616 Sunset Blvd., Los Angeles, CA   90028
(323) 467–4242 • fax: (323) 467–3720
e-mail: humanrights@cchr.org
Web site: www.cchr.org

CCHR is a nonprofit organization whose goal is to expose and eradicate criminal acts and human rights abuses by psychiatry. The organization believes that psychiatric drugs, including some antidepressants, can cause serious mental health problems and violence. The CCHR publishes numerous books, including *Psyched Out* and *The Cloning of the American Mind.*

Depression and Bipolar Support Alliance
730 N. Franklin St., Ste. 501, Chicago, IL   60610
(312) 642–0049 • fax: (312) 642–7243
e-mail: info@dbsalliance.org
Web site: www.ndma.org

The DBSA provides support and advocacy for patients with depression and bipolar disorder. It seeks to educate the public about the biochemical nature of these illnesses and to end the stigmatization of those who suffer from them. The alliance publishes the books *The Anti-Depressant Sourcebooks* and *Breaking the Patterns of Depression,* among others.

International Foundation for Research and Education on Depression (iFred)
2017-D Renard Ct., Annapolis, MD
(410) 268–0044 • fax: (443) 782–0739
e-mail: info@ifred.org
Web site: www.ifred.org

iFred is a nonprofit organization that seeks to bring information on depression to patients in the public in a positive, encouraging manner. The group's goal is to change the way in which depression and mental illness are viewed in society by celebrating individuals' ability to recover and move forward. iFred publishes facts and advice about depression on its Web site.

National Alliance for the Mentally Ill
2107 Wilson Blvd., Ste. 300, Arlington, VA   22201
(703) 524–7600 • fax: (703) 524–9094
Web site: www.nami.org

NAMI is a consumer advocacy and support organization composed largely of family members of people with severe mental illness, including depression. The alliance adheres to the position that severe mental illnesses are biological brain diseases and that mentally ill people should not be blamed for their condition. Its publications include the bimonthly newsletter *NAMI Advocate* and the book *I Am Not Sick, I Don't Need Help!*

National Institute of Mental Health
6001 Executive Blvd., Bethesda, MD 20892
(301) 443–4513 • fax: (301) 443–4279
e-mail: nimhinfo@nih.gov
Web site: www.nimh.nih.gov

The NIMH is part of the National Institutes of Health, a division of the federal government's Department of Health and Human Services. It commissions and funds research on mental health issues and supports the training of mental health professionals. NIMH publishes numerous reports and booklets every year, such as *In Harm's Way: Suicide in America*, as well as maintaining an extensive educational Web site.

National Mental Health Association
2001 N. Beauregard St., 12th Fl., Alexandria, VA 22511
(703) 684–7722 • fax: (703) 684–5968
Web site: www.nmha.org

The NMHA is a nonprofit organization that focuses on broad goals associated with advancing awareness of general mental health issues. It works to educate the public about mental illness and its effects, treatments, and prevention by holding public awareness campaigns and programs and sponsoring projects by other nonprofit groups. The NMHA publishes a quarterly newsletter, *The Bell.*

Suicide Awareness Voices of Education (SAVE)
9001 E. Bloomington Fwy., Ste. 150
Bloomington, MN 55420
(952) 946–7998
Web site: www.save.org

SAVE is a nonprofit organization founded by suicide survivors whose mission focuses on education about suicide prevention. The group also works to reduce the stigma associated with suicide and provide support for suicide survivors and their families. SAVE publishes a semi-annual newsletter, *Voices of Save*.

United States Food and Drug Administration
5600 Fishers Ln., Rockville, MD   20857
(888) 463–6332
Web site: www.fda.gov

As the agency of the U.S. government charged with protecting the health of the public against impure and unsafe food, drugs, cosmetics, and other potential hazards, the FDA is the agency that approves the use of antidepressants and issues public advisories about their use. It publishes the *FDA Consumer* magazine.

World Federation for Mental Health
6564 Loisdale Ct., Ste. 301, Springfield, VA   22150
(703) 313–8680 • fax: (703) 313–8683
e-mail: info@wfmh.com
Web site: www.wmfh.com

The federation is dedicated to improving public mental health worldwide and strives to coordinate mental health organizations and enhance mental health care in developing countries. The WFMH publishes the *World Federation for Mental Health Newsletter* quarterly.

Bibliography

Books

Daniel G. Amen — *Healing Anxiety and Depression.* Berkeley, CA: Berkeley Trade, 2004.

Shoshanna Bennett — *Beyond the Blues: A Guide to Understanding and Treating Prenatal and Postpartum Depression.* San Jose, CA: Moodswings Press, 2003.

J. Raymond DePaulo — *Understanding Depression: What We Know and What You Can Do About It.* Sydney: Wiley, 2003.

Kitty Dukakis and Larry Tye — *Shock: The Healing Power of Electroconvulsive Therapy.* New York: Penguin, 2006.

Peter D. Kramer — *Against Depression.* New York: Penguin, 2006.

H.E. Logue — *Fly Me to the Moon: Bipolar Journey through Mania and Depression.* Parker, CO: Outskirts Press, 2006.

Lisa Machoian — *The Disappearing Girl: Learning the Language of Teenage Depression.* New York: Dutton, 2005.

Richard O'Connor — *Undoing Perpetual Stress: The Missing Connection Between Depression, Anxiety and 21st Century Illness.* New York: Berkeley Publishing Group, 2005.

Steven C. Schachter and Dieter Schmidt, eds.	*Vagus Nerve Stimulation.* London: Taylor & Francis, 2003.
David Servan-Schreiber	*The Instinct to Heal: Curing Stress, Anxiety, and Depression Without Drugs and Without Talk Therapy.* New York: Rodale, 2004.
Brooke Shields	*Down Came the Rain: My Journey Through Postpartum Depression.* New York: Hyperion, 2005.
Daniel N. Stern	*The Present Moment in Psychotherapy and Everyday Life.* New York: W.W. Norton & Co., 2004.
Andrew L. Stoll	*The Omega-3 Connection: The Groundbreaking Anti-Depression Diet and Brain Program.* New York: Simon & Schuster 2001.
Michael E. Thase	*Beating the Blues: New Approaches to Overcoming Dysthymia and Chronic Mild Depression.* Oxford: Oxford University Press, 2004.
Tracy Thompson	*The Ghost in the House: Motherhood, Raising Children, and Struggling with Depression.* New York: HarperCollins, 2006.
Njemile Zakiya	*A Peek Inside the Goo: Depression and the Borderline Personality.* Schenectady, NY: Asabi Publishing, 2006.

Periodicals

Patricia Anstett — "Ray of Hope: More Help Available for Seasonal Affective Disorder Sufferers," *Detroit Free Press*, November 28, 2006.

Sandra G. Boodman — "Sick of Expectations," *Washington Post*, August 1, 2006.

Jane E. Brody — "Shock Therapy Loses Some of Its Shock Value," *New York Times*, September 19, 2006.

Daniel J. Carlat — "Vagus Nerve Stimulation and Depression: Conflict of Interest's 'Perfect Storm,'" *Psychiatric Times*, December 2006.

Marilyn Elias — "Conquering Depression Can Take Many Treatments," *USA Today*, November 1, 2006.

Joe Fahy — "Out of the Shadows," *Pittsburgh Post-Gazette*, October 18, 2006.

Barnaby J. Feder — "Battle Lines in Treating Depression," *New York Times*, September 10, 2006.

Dennis Fiely — "Teen Depression," *Columbus Dispatch*, October 2, 2006.

Max Fink — "Should the Diagnosis of Melancholia Be Revived?" *Psychiatric Times*, June 1, 2006.

Harvard Mental Health Letter — "Electroconvulsive Therapy," February 2007.

Mary Ann Hughes   "The Two Faces of Mental Illness," *Library Journal*, May 1, 2004.

Dafna Izenberg   "Does Therapy Belong in Class?" *Maclean's*, January 1, 2007.

Avery Johnson   "Targeting Depression," *Wall Street Journal*, December 14, 2006.

Barbara Kiser   "The Dreamcatcher," *New Scientist*, April 12, 2003.

Gogo Lidz   "My Adventures in Psychopharmacology," *New York*, January 8, 2007.

Mental Health Weekly   , "FDA Extends Suicide Warning to Antidepressants for Young Adults," December 18, 2006.

Michael Craig Miller   "Minds and Magnets," *Newsweek*, December 11, 2006.

Cole Moreton   "Children on the Couch," *London Independent*, October 8, 2006.

Kate Murphy   "Easing Depression Without Drugs," *Business Week*, May 2, 2005.

Kim Painter   "Well Beyond 'Baby Blues,'" *USA Today*, September 11, 2006.

Rita Rubin   "Moms Pass Depression On to Kids," *USA Today*, March 22, 2006.

Susan Saulny   "A Legacy of the Storm: Depression and Suicide," *New York Times*, June 21, 2006.

Nancy Shute   "Teens, Drugs, and Sadness," *U.S. News and World Report*, August 30, 2004.

Maia Szalavitz   "The K Fix," *New Scientist*, January 20, 2007.

Curtis L. Taylor   "Too Manly for Depression," *Newsday*, October 24, 2006.

Robert   "Campus Psychiatry Comes Clean,"
VerBruggen   *American Spectator*, December 6, 2006.

Index

A

Acupuncture, 109
Alchemy, 32
Alcohol/drug abuse
    in dysthymia, 27–28
    as mask for depression in
      men, 21
    as warning sign of suicide, 57
Alzheimer's disease, 44–45
    depression and brain changes
      in, 41
*American Journal of Preventive
Medicine,* 105
American Journal of Psychiatry,
112, 158
The Anatomy of Melancholy
(Burton), 11, 33, 36
Anhedonia, 25
Antidepressants, 140–141
    account of therapy with,
      77–85
    clinical trials of, 152–153
    dual-action of, 29, 150, 157
    problem with delayed action
      of, 143–145
    psychotherapy in conjunction
      with, 107–108
    worldwide market for, 148
    youth suicide and, 155–160
    See also Selective serotonin
      reuptake inhibitors (SSRIs)
Anxiety disorders, 118
Anxiety neurosis, 142
Archives of General Psychiatry
(journal), 107
Aretaeus of Cappadocia, 31–32
Ayd, Frank, 140

B

B vitamins, 110, 111
Bennett, Shoshana, 61, 65–66
Benzodiazepines, 137–140
Berger, Frank, 136
Biological Psychiatry (journal), 107,
129
Bipolar disorder (manic-depressive
illness), 17
Brain
    changes in, Alzheimer's
      disease/depression, 41, 44
    of child vs. adult, 156–157
    deep stimulation of, 97–102
    PET scans showing changes
      from psychotherapy vs.
      medication, 119
    transcranial magnetic stimula-
      tion in the, 127–132
Burton, Robert, 11, 33, 35–36, 37
Buspirone (BuSpar), 140, 149

C

Children
    brain of, vs. adult, 156–157
    depression in, 22–23
Corticotropin releasing factor
    (CRF) antagonists, 151
Couples therapy, 117–118
Creativity
    depression associated with, 10
    disease and, 165–167
Cymbalta, 150, 156–157

D

David, 35, 36
Deep brain stimulation, personal
    account of, 97–102

Defeat Depression campaign, 142

Department of Health and Human Services, U.S. (DDHS), 106

Depression
  biochemistry of, 42–44
  campaigns for awareness of, 142–143
  causes of, 19
  controversy over medication for, 161–169
  first recognized as medical condition, 11
  in history, 31–39
  prevalence of, 10, 15, 42
  as risk factor for physical illnesses, 12, 41–42

Depressive disorders, forms of, 16–17

Depressive personality disorder, 26

Descartes, Rene, 32

DeWine, Mike, 56

Diabetologia (journal), 41

Diagnostic and Statistical Manual of Mental Disorders (DSM-III, American Psychiatric Association), 141–142

Diaries (Kierkegaard), 163–164

Diet, mental wellness and, 110–111

Dietary supplements, 106–107

Dinesen, Isak, 165, 167

Docosahexanaenoic acid (DHA), 121

Domenici, Pete, 47–48

Dysthymia, 16
  causes of, 27–28
  drugs vs. psychotherapy in, 29–30
  prevalence of, 25–26
  treatment for, 28–29

E

Eaton, Joseph, 38

Eicosapentaenoic acid (EPA), 111

Elderly
  depression in, 21–22
  psychotherapy for late-life depression in, 22

Electroconvulsive therapy, 130

Esquirol, Jean-Philipe, 34

Evans, Dwight, 12

exercise, 105–106

F

Family therapy, 117

Farley, Peter, 12

Fluoxetine (Prozac), 146
  See also Selective serotonin reuptake inhibitors (SSRIs)

Food and Drug Administration, U.S. (FDA), 157

Freud, Sigmund, 38, 135

G

Garrett Lee Smith Memorial Act (2004), 48, 49

Gauguin, Paul, 166

Glenmullen, Joseph, 158

Group therapy, 117

H

Heart disease, 43–44

Hippocrates, 11, 31

Hoerhaave, Herman, 32

Homeopathy, 108–109

Humors, 31, 32

I

Illness as Metaphor (Sontag), 166

Infanticide, 62

International Classification of Diseases, 66

J

Job, 36–37
Johnson, Samuel, 34
Journal of Affective Disorders, 112
Journal of Clinical Psychopharmacology, 106–107, 108
Journal of the American College of Cardiology, 43
Judd, Lew, 142

K

Kennedy, Ted, 55
Kielholz, Paul, 140
Kierkegaard, Søren, 163–164

L

Librium, 137
Light therapy, 111–112
Listening to Prozac (Kramer), 167

M

Meditation, 112–113
Melancholia, 31, 32, 33
Men, depression in, 20–21
Mended Hearts, 44
Meprobamate (Miltown), 136
Massage therapy, 109
Mood, disturbances of, 26–27
Movement Disorders (journal), 101
Moyer, Jennifer, 59–60, 66–67

N

Napier, Richard, 32
National Depressive and Manic Depressive Association, 30

National Institutes of Mental Health (NIMH), 10, 20, 23
Neurotransmitters
    antidepressants and, 108, 150
    exercise and, 105
    methods to increase levels of, 109, 110, 112
New Scientist (magazine), 12
Nickles, Don, 47
Nietzsche, Friedrich, 166

O

Omega-3 fatty acids, 110, 111, 120–124
    dosage of, for depression, 124–126
Omega-6 fatty acids, 121

P

Personality, dysthymia and, 26
Physical illness
    depression as, 10
    depression as risk factor for, 12
    in patients with dysthymia, 27–28
    role of depression in, 12, 40–45
Placebo effect, 152
Plath, Sylvia, 143
Postpartum depression, 20, 59
    causes of, 62–64
    identifying symptoms of, 60–61
    personal account of, 69–76
    personal/societal pressures and, 64–65
    postpartum psychosis vs., 61–62
Postpartum Support International (PSI), 63

posttraumatic stress disorder (PTSD), 118

Premenstrual syndrome (PMS), 20

Prozac Backlash (Glenmullen), 158

Prozac (fluoxetine). *See* Fluoxetine; Selective serotonin reuptake inhibitors

Psychodynamic therapy, 115–116

Psychotherapy/talk therapy, 22

    in conjunction with antidepressants, 107–108

    for late-life depression in elderly, 22

    varieties of, 114–119

R

Recognizing the Depressed Patient (Ayd), 140

Reid, Harry, 47

Religious melancholy, 34–35, 37–38

Research Units on Pediatric Psychopharmacology (RUPPs), 23

Rubin, J.H., 37

S

S-adenocylmethione (SAMe), 106–107

Saul, 35

Schildkrout, Joseph, 11

Selective serotonin reuptake inhibitors (SSRIs), 11, 28–29, 148

    delayed action of, 144–145

    marketing of, 141

    mechanism of, 157

    use in children, 147

Serotonin, 106, 108

    antidepressants and, 149, 150

    exercise and levels of, 105

    methods to increase levels of, 109, 110

    SSRIs and, 157

Shepard, Michael, 141

Smith, Garrett Lee, 46–47, 50–55

Smith, Gordon, 46–47, 49–50, 58

Smith, Sharon, 48, 49–50, 53, 56–58

Sontag, Susan, 166

spirituality

    in treatment of depression, 109–110

    See also Religious melancholy

SSRIs. *See* Selective serotonin reuptake inhibitors

St. John's wort *(Hypericum perforation)*, 108

Stress hormones

    depression and, 42–43

    research in antagonists of, 151

Substance P, 151–152

Suicide

    debate over link between antidepressants and, 153

    delay in antidepressant action and, 144–145

    link between depression and, 46

    as major cause of deaths among youths, 49

    warning signs of, 57

    youth, SSRIs and, 147

Support groups, 118

Symptoms

    of depression, 17–18

    of dysthymia, 25

    of major depression, 16

    of mania, 17–18

    of postpartum depression, 60–61

T

Talk therapy. *See* Psychotherapy/
   talk therapy
TeenScreen, 56
Thyroid disease, postpartum de-
   pression and, 63–64
Tranquilizers, 136–140
Transcranial magnetic stimulation,
   127–132
Treatment
   alternative, 104–113
   of postpartum depression, 65
   reluctance to seek, 15–16, 30
   See also Antidepressants;
      Psychotherapy/talk therapy
Tricyclic antidepressants, 29, 140,
   147
   SSRIs vs., 149

U

Uridine, 110
U.S. News and World Report
   (magazine), 12

V

Vagus nerve stimulation, 130
Valium, 137

W

Weil, Robert, 38
Willis, Thomas, 41
Women
   depression in, 20
   See also Postpartum depres-
      sion

Y

Yates, Andrea, 60, 62
Yoga, 112–113
Youth
   account of depression in,
      86–96
   SSRIs and suicide in, 147
   suicide as major cause of
      deaths among, 49